Robert Kelly SJ

WITH GOD ON OUR SIDE

D1079947

VERITAS

First published 1995 by
Veritas Publications
7-8 Lower Abbey Street
Dublin 1

ISBN 1 85390 263 2

British Library Cataloguing
in Publication Data.
A catalogue record for
this book is available
from the British Library.

Cover design by Bill Bolger
Printed in the Republic of Ireland by Betaprint Ltd, Dublin.

CONTENTS

INTRODUCTION

'The life you have is hidden with Christ in God.' In this book I offer some reflections on the hidden life of Christ and on the wonder and mystery of the hidden life of each person. I would like to start in what may seem a strange place – a modern supermarket. Over the years, as I came back to Ireland on leave from missionary work in Africa, I noticed how my attitude to supermarkets was changing. In the early years, coming from poorly-stocked shops in Zambia, a visit to an Irish supermarket was like a visit to wonderland. I delighted in the abundance and variety of goods offered and bought too easily. As years passed and the shops in Zambia became poorer and the gap between the economies grew, I began to react quite differently. When I came on leave, I now went to the supermarket with a different, more detached spirit. I walked round with a sense of uneasiness at the affluence of the big stores, tinged, I confess with shame, with a sense of superiority that I could resist the inclination to buy.

Most people, I think, are aware of the danger and the power of consumerism, of how we can be manipulated by modern advertising into buying what we do not need. But I think there is a more subtle and serious danger, namely that the consumer society and the advertising world could dictate not just my sense of values regarding what I need and should buy, but could even dictate a sense of my own personal value. They could suggest that I am what I can buy and what I have, and that the more I can succeed and can earn and spend, then the greater will be my feeling of self-worth. This mentality is, of course, strongly reinforced by the media world which constantly holds up for my admiration the great and successful of the world, the heroes of sport, politics, business and entertainment. These are the people who make the headlines. And, even though in quieter moments I can tell myself that all this glamour, wealth, notoriety and success does not confer happiness, I still feel that my own daily, humdrum life is a somewhat poor and mediocre affair.

I believe that we really have to make an effort to resist the influence of the media and not allow them to decide for us what gives value and meaning to life. We must not allow the daily media propaganda to dictate our sense of values and, above all, we must not allow it to dictate our identity. The media observe and report on the externals and surface of life. They emphasise the appearances, the exciting, the transient. The lives of the vast majority of people are hidden and humble and do not attract media attention. That does not mean that such lives have little meaning or worth or are in any sense unimportant. Our faith asks us to look below the surface and not to judge by appearances. It invites us to look at what the camera cannot see, to look beneath the externals and become aware of the wonder, value and beauty of each unique person, no matter how obscure or hidden his or her life is.

In a certain city there was a well-known curio shop. It drew many customers because of the great variety of strange and wonderful objects and artefacts gathered from many cultures and periods of history. There were ancient carvings, exotic masks, human and animal skeletons, strange statues, old maps, guns, spears, coins. It was like a small museum. The owner was a little old man who sat on a high stool behind the counter. He enjoyed the sense of wonder on the faces of the customers who browsed in his shop. One day an over-awed customer came up and said it was the best-stocked curio-shop he had ever seen in all his travels. He then asked the owner, 'What in your opinion is the most interesting, strange and wonderful object in this shop?' The little old man paused, then smiled and said, 'Surely the most wonderful and fascinating thing in this shop is myself!'

Our faith would say Amen to that story. Our faith asks each of us to believe that our world became a more wonderful and beautiful place on the day we were born, because in our birth something more of the mystery and beauty of God was revealed to the world. If we see ourselves through the eyes of the media, we can appear small, dull and insignificant. But through the eyes of faith we see ourselves as full of mystery, wonder and beauty, made in the image and likeness of God, the source of all beauty and love. Our lives are the most amazing love stories, full of extraordinary wonder and beauty, more incredible than any sensational tabloid romance. God has never given an interview to any reporter armed with camera and tape-recorder, but he has spoken through prophets and through his Son and through them has revealed the inside story of the deep hidden meaning and beauty of the life of each one of us.

There is nothing superficial or transient about those lives. Both in their origin and destiny they are touched by eternity. To

Jeremiah and to each of us God says, 'Before I formed you in the womb, I knew you' (Jr 1:5). God has always wanted us. Paul speaks the same truth and links our destiny with Christ. 'Before the world was made, God chose us, chose us in Christ, to live through love in his presence, to become his adopted children through Jesus Christ. It is in him that we were claimed as God's own, chosen from the beginning' (Ep 1:3-12). We are older than we think! Yet we are eternally young with Christ.

In Richard Bach's lovely fantasy, *There's No Such Place as Far Away*, the birds are the philosophers who comment on the deep meaning of life. The author is going to visit his young friend Rae to celebrate her birthday. Part of his trip is with the Eagle who asks what a birthday is and what it means to celebrate a birthday. The author explains, 'That means we are going to celebrate the hour that Rae began to be and before which she was not.' To this the eagle replies, 'A time before Rae's life began! Don't you think rather that it is Rae's life that began before time ever was?' It seems that poets, humorists and inspired prophets all agree that great mystery surrounds each person.

When we speak of the 'mystery' of each person, we are not suggesting something which cannot be understood or which lacks meaning. Mystery does not suggest absence of meaning but rather a meaning so rich and profound that it cannot be understood quickly. Time is needed, prayer is needed if we are to explore the wonder and beauty of that life of each person which is hidden with Christ in God. And so, this book, which is about the mystery of the hidden life of Christ and the hidden life of each person, is also a book about prayer.

1

AN EXTRAORDINARY CHOICE

Jesus was about thirty-three years of age when he was crucified. Out of thirty-three years spent on this earth as a man, only three were devoted to an active public ministry. Thirty years were lived in obscurity, a hidden life in a hidden village called Nazareth. In our prayer and reflection we usually pass quickly over these long, hidden years to concentrate on his public life, his teaching and miracles, his passion and death, and his founding of a new community of love. I suggest we pause and reflect on this extraordinary choice to live thirty years in hiddenness and obscurity. I believe it has much to tell us about God and his ways, about ourselves and the true meaning and wonder of our lives, and about how those lives can find their most meaningful fulfilment no matter how hidden and ordinary they may seem by the world's standards.

The first thing we must stress about the hidden life of Jesus is that it was a choice made by God. We are not talking of chance but of deliberate choice. God chooses to have it this way and so he is saying something to us by this extraordinary choice. I say 'extraordinary' choice, for it must surely seem so to our way of thinking. Let us ask what Jesus has come to do. He has come to save a world which has waited long years for a Messiah. He has come to inaugurate God's kingdom of love here on earth, to call all to repentance, to abolish fear, to break the power of Satan and sin. What an agenda! He has thirty-three years to accomplish this mighty programme. Out of these he spends thirty in hidden, ordinary daily living. During those hidden years he does none of the things we would expect him to do with a view to his main purpose in coming. He does not gather disciples, he does not open a school, he does not write or study, he works no miracles, he does not confront oppressive political or religious structures.

This is a deliberate choice and covers thirty out of thirty-three years of his precious human life. Are we to say this is not significant? Is this choice not full of meaning? Is he not already teaching us here something of fundamental importance? Is he not already in a hidden but true way saving us all? He is teaching us what we find so hard to learn: that God's ways are not ours, that God's values are not our values. Jesus is trying to open our eyes to God and his ways and his values, to the wonder and beauty of simple, hidden, humble things. If we are honest, we must admit that we find God's choice very strange. It amazes us, even shocks us. Something inside us judges this choice and says it is not wise, it is a waste of valuable time.

How do we think Jesus should have used these years? How would we give meaning and value to those thirty years? We would suggest long-term planning, surveys, fund-raising, programmes. We always want something we can see and measure. These are our value norms and criteria. Perhaps the message of the hidden years is an invitation to revise our criteria of what gives value, meaning and worth to life. Because this is such a hard lesson for us to learn, Jesus devoted thirty years to teaching it, not by words but simply by living it. He invites us to go deeper into the meaning of human life and seek its value, wonder and beauty at a deeper level than activity and achievement.

We are all familiar with the four gospels of Matthew, Mark, Luke and John. We may not have seen but have probably heard of certain writings called the Apocrypha. These were religious writings in circulation in the early Christian Church. Some of these were called 'gospels' and dealt with the life and teaching of Jesus. The early Church, guided by the Holy Spirit, identified Matthew, Mark, Luke and John as the authentic inspired gospels. The Apocrypha were not accepted as inspired scripture on which we could safely base our faith. They were pious literature containing beautiful stories and legends. It is interesting to note that they contain stories of miraculous happenings in the hidden life of Jesus in Nazareth. We can see here our human resistance to what is ordinary, daily and humdrum, our impatience with what is routine and uneventful. We want the extraordinary. We crave signs, wonders and miracles. God in Jesus invites us to resist this very human tendency, to look at life with his eyes and so discover the true miracle and beauty hidden in ordinary daily life.

One of the miracle stories found in the apocryphal gospels goes like this. Jesus as a young boy is playing with friends, making clay birds out of mud. It is innocent fun but unfortunately it is the Sabbath and making clay birds could be classed as work! Therefore he was breaking the Sabbath. A passing Pharisee admonishes the youngsters for breaking the Sabbath. Sitting on the ground, the boy Jesus looks up at the disapproving elder and then at the clay birds. Then with a smile on his young muddy face he claps his hands and the clay birds come to life and fly off into the blue sky! This is a lovely story, but not part of the inspired gospel. The gospel gives us the good news which, in its own way, is incredibly more miraculous and wonderful, namely that Jesus who is the Son of God lived for thirty years such a hidden life that he was totally indistinguishable from the ordinary folk of the village of Nazareth. It is this that will cause wonder, even scandal, later on. They will say to one another, 'How did he learn to read? He has not been taught' (Jn 7:15). And again they will ask, 'What is this wisdom that has been granted him, and these miracles that are worked through him? This is the carpenter, surely, the son of Mary' (Mk 6:3). They only saw a carpenter all through those years in Nazareth. But God saw his beloved Son in whom he was well-pleased. Jesus asks us to look at ourselves and one another with God's eyes.

In his letter to the Corinthians, St Paul reflects on another extraordinary choice made by God in Jesus, the choice of walking the road of compassion for the poor and sinners, a road that led to Calvary and crucifixion. Paul speaks bluntly here and says what the world thinks of this choice and the shameful death it involved. He says it was by our standards weakness and foolishness. 'And so, while the Jews demand miracles and the Greeks look for wisdom, here are we preaching a crucified Christ; to the Jews an obstacle they cannot get over, to the pagans madness, but to those who have been called, whether they are Jews or Greeks, a Christ who is the power and wisdom of God. For God's foolishness is wiser than human wisdom, and God's weakness is stronger than human strength' (I Co 1:22-25).

Can we not say the same about the choice to remain hidden in Nazareth for thirty years? We would say it was another kind of foolishness and waste in view of the world's need and the urgency of salvation. But how wise and truly caring is our God. Does he not read and understand our true needs? We need to know that our humble lives have meaning and value. Is God's hiddenness not more beautiful, more approachable and lifegiving than the bright glare of publicity that would surround miracles and wonders? Surely, again, God's foolishness is wiser than our wisdom. Without saying a word, Jesus teaches us where real meaning and beauty are to be found. They are not found in glamour, notoriety and success.

The wisdom of the world glorifies these criteria and pays homage to its VIPs. But most people live hidden, humble and obscure lives. No one knows about them, nor cares. But God knows every detail of their lives and truly cares. The Psalmist speaks of that total and intimate knowledge God has of our every thought, word and movement (Ps 139). The knowledge described in the psalm is the knowledge that comes from loving. It is not knowledge that comes from watching, spying or supervising. It is the knowledge that comes from caring and loving, the knowledge parents have of their children, the knowledge lovers have of each other. Sometimes we have the mistaken notion that we must pray to attract God's attention. Jesus tells us we are the objects of God's loving attention every single moment of our ordinary daily life.

2

TREASURE WITHIN US

St Paul's great words about our salvation are very well known, that Jesus Christ the Son of God loved us and gave his life for us (Ga 2:20). We always apply these words, and rightly so, to the supreme act of love on Calvary. Can we not now also apply them to the hidden life of Nazareth? There also, Jesus Christ the Son of God gave his life for us. His long hidden life of thirty years was given for us to rescue us from feeling small and meaningless, to remind us of our true identity, to tell us we are beautiful and precious to God. Can we not say that he has already begun to save us by this choice of the hidden life of Nazareth? He is saving us in an unexpected way and saving us from an enemy that we ourselves had not identified, that subtle and destructive enemy that suggests that our lives are trivial and have little meaning or importance, that enemy that wants to deny that we are made in the very image and likeness of God.

The hidden life of Nazareth, which looks like foolishness and waste in our eyes, reveals the wisdom and love of God. When Jesus chose to spend thirty out of thirty-three years of his life on earth in a hidden village, he was identifying with the vast majority of the human race whose stories never make the news and who live and die in obscurity. Let us now explore that wisdom even more deeply so that we do not lose the true richness and beauty of this revelation. It could be misunderstood. Let us be clear about what we are not saying. We are not saying that since most of us do not rise to greatness and fame, then we should make the most of our humble situation, that we should turn necessity into virtue and be like Jesus who was patient with hiddenness and humility through those years hidden in Nazareth. We are not saying this.

We are saying something much deeper, something incredibly more wonderful and beautiful. We repeat that the hidden life of Nazareth was a deliberate choice. God in Jesus made this choice, in order to invite us to look deeper into reality, into the mystery of being, the meaning of life. God is not saying in a condescending way, 'Since most people live hidden ordinary lives, I too will choose such a life to console them.' No! Our God is not condescending in this sense. God is love and shares all. What God is saying in Jesus is this: 'There is no such thing as an ordinary human life. Each person is created in the image of God and is a unique and beautiful reflection of God. Each single person is called to fullness of life, to beauty and to meaning, and is called to begin this experience right now in this life, no matter how humble his or her circumstances.'

Jesus later describes his mission in these words: 'I have come that they may have life and have it to the full' (Jn 10:10). Jesus has come to give this fullness of life to all and to show us where to look for it. His long, hidden life is a dramatic protest against our tendency to look in the wrong place and to link meaning and fullness of life with wealth and achievement. Jesus is trying to tell us that each person is uniquely beautiful and precious and lovable before God, no matter what the external circumstances of his or hers may be.

Jesus did not come to ask us to make the best of a bad situation, to be patient with this humble life because there is a better one to come. He invites us to live in the present, to find fullness of life right now and just where we are. He invites us to identify and choose with him what is true and lasting treasure. He asks us to accept the gift he brings, the amazing grace of God's love which gives true meaning to life. He invites us to resist the compulsions of our time – the tendency to judge by appearances, to equate value and meaning with possessions, fame, success, to compare myself and my status with others who appear to have it made, thus allowing myself to feel inferior. He asks us to look at life with God's eyes. The invitation is for all and perhaps especially for those who may seem to have it made and who could be in danger of losing their own deepest and truest, most beautiful selves.

Some philosophers tell us that happiness lies not in acquiring goods and possessions, but rather in realising what we do not need. Socrates believed that the truly wise person would lead a frugal life. This same philosopher was often seen in the market-place. People were surprised, and when they asked him why, he would answer, 'I like to walk around among these stalls and see all the things I am happy without!' There is wisdom in this answer and a large amount of self-discipline. But this is not what we are talking about. We are talking not about self-discipline but about love.

Jesus is not a philosopher offering us an ideology that will lead us to self-mastery. Jesus comes to offer us life, meaning, treasure and fulfilment. He tells us we do not have to go to the supermarket to find it nor do we need money to buy it. What he offers is a gift: grace, amazing grace. In one image he compares it to a spring of water welling up inside, a source of freshness, new life, growth. 'If you only knew what God is offering and who it is that is saying to you: "Give me a drink", you would have been the one to ask, and he would have given you living water' (Jn 4:10). It is only when we become aware of this life, this treasure within us, that we shall be able to resist the compulsions of our time. We must have wealth within us, if we are to resist the attraction of wealth outside us. It is not a matter of self-discipline. It is a question of accepting a gift, of accepting a love offered freely without condition. Prayer is one place where we can joyfully accept the gift. When we are sure of this inner gift of love nourishing and renewing us, then we may begin to live more from the inside out and be less under the domination of the externals of modern life, the advertising propaganda and the slogans of the present moment. We must experience true inner life if we are not to be deceived by the many counterfeits around us.

If we accept God's gift, which is nothing less than Jesus himself, then our hearts can become his Nazareth. He wants to live there and share our hidden lives. St Paul uses an expressive word to describe the effect on our lives when we accept Jesus. He says, 'For anyone who is in Christ there is a new creation' (II Co 5:17). The expression 'new creation' emphasises the idea of gift. In our first creation we received life as a total gift. All we had to do was accept. So Jesus, our new life, is a total gift. It has nothing to do with our worthiness, but everything to do with his love. His loving presence within us is not a reward for our observance of his laws but simply a pure gift. If we accept all as a gift, we can experience a new sense of joy and life which no money can buy. It is a share in Jesus' very own joy, the joy he experienced in knowing his Father's love. 'I have told you this so that my own joy may be in you and your joy may be complete' (Jn 15:11).

In the story of the Prodigal Son, Jesus describes the welcome experienced by the young son who returns to his father in repentance. The boy had run away from the boredom of the hidden life on the farm to experience the life and happiness that money could buy. He returns empty and disillusioned. He is welcomed with a loving embrace and given the best robe in the house and a ring and sandals and his father organises a celebration with music and feasting. When the house became quiet that night after the party, I suspect that the young man took a long time to get to sleep. And I am sure that what filled his mind and heart was not the beautiful robe hanging at the end of the bed nor the ring and sandals, but the memory of the loving embrace of his father. That boy could tell us what it means to become a 'new creation'. Can I share that experience? All I have to do is believe that God my Father is love, and arise in my heart and go to him and accept his embrace. I can do that right now in prayer.

3

THE DIVINE CONNECTION

St John describes Jesus as the Word of God. He is God's Word made flesh (Jn 1:14). In his public life, people will be amazed at his teaching and will wonder where he got such wisdom. They will exclaim, 'There has never been anybody who has spoken like him' (Jn 7:46). After he preached in the synagogue, we are told that, 'They were astonished by the gracious words that came from his lips' (Lk 4:21). Yet for thirty years that voice remained silent. In the gospels we have only one recorded sentence spoken by Jesus in those thirty years. But in that one sentence we have a precious clue as to what gave meaning to his life and what should give meaning to our lives. It is in the mystery suggested by that one utterance that we must look for an answer to the most basic question of the human heart: has life any real meaning?

It is St Luke who, for a brief moment, draws back the curtain which covers the hidden life of Jesus in Nazareth. We get a glimpse of the Holy Family making a pilgrimage to Jerusalem. An incident is recorded and then the curtain falls again. Our chief interest here is in the one sentence spoken by the young Jesus in that recorded incident. Mary and Joseph make the annual pilgrimage to Jerusalem to celebrate the Passover. Jesus, now twelve years of age, accompanies them for the first time. When the celebrations are over, the pilgrims set out for home but the boy Jesus goes missing. Mary and Joseph search for him, eventually finding him in the temple talking to the doctors of the Law. When they complain and tell him of their anxiety, he answers, 'Did you not know that I must be busy with my Father's affairs?' (Lk 2:49). We are told that Mary and Joseph did not understand. We should not be surprised. Here we are being introduced by Jesus into the mystery that he who is the son of Mary is also the Son of God.

This first recorded word of Jesus speaks of his Father and thus introduces us to a new and deeper hidden life of Jesus. We have been speaking of his hidden life, meaning that he, the Messiah, by living as a village carpenter, is unknown to the great world outside Nazareth. But we are now led into an even more hidden reality of vastly greater significance, into a place of mystery and beauty where we are privileged to be shown that which is the very mainspring of the life of Jesus: his relationship of deep, warm, personal love with his Father, God. Later, in his public life, he will speak often of his Father and their mutual love. This love is the source of all his joy and comfort. 'I am not alone. The one who sent me is with me' (Jn 8:16). His miracles of compassion have their source in this love. 'The Father who is the source of life has made the Son the source of life' (Jn 5:26). His words of wisdom come from the Father. 'He whom God has sent speaks God's own words. The Father loves the Son and has entrusted everything to him' (Jn 3:33). This love gave all meaning to his life and even to his death. This love, which he so often spoke about with such warmth in his public life, was the deep hidden current that flowed beneath the surface of that otherwise totally uneventful life of thirty years in Nazareth. Truly his real life was hidden with God.

We are not mere spectators of this great love story. We are drawn intimately into this flow of life and love. All this is for us. When Jesus has completed the work of our salvation entrusted to him by the Father and appears to Mary Magdalene on the first Easter Sunday morning, he asks her to bring this good news to the disciples: 'Go and tell them I am ascending to my Father and to your Father' (Jn 20:17). We have the same Father as Jesus and all that was true for Jesus is equally true for us. Each of us is loved by that Father in the same way that Jesus is loved. 'I have made your name known to them, so that the love with which you loved me may be in them and so that I may be in them' (Jn 17:26). Our deepest life too must be 'hidden with Christ in God'. It is here we must find our identity and the answer to the question,'has life any real meaning?' We can now dare to say that our lives have the same deep and beautiful meaning as that of Jesus. The Spirit of Jesus which called out Abba to God is given to us 'and it makes us cry out Abba, Father! The Spirit himself and our spirit bear united witness that we are children of God' (Rm 8:16).

'Did you not know that I must be busy with my Father's affairs?' (Lk 2:49). Jesus is the son of Mary and Joseph but he is not their property. He belongs to God. This is true of each of us. We are not the property of our parents. We belong to God. The Psalmist reminds us of the mystery of our origins: 'It was you who created my inmost self and put me together in my mother's womb' (Ps 139:13). And St Paul tells us that Christ was involved in this mystery. 'Before the world was made, God chose us, chose us in Christ' (Ep 1:4). Note that we are eternally chosen in Christ. It is only through Jesus that we can experience the truth of our divine origin and know our true identity. In Christ God embraces our humanity. We can say Jesus is our guarantee that we can trust the good news of our true meaning, value and worth before God. It is hard to accept the wonder of our own being, our own amazing importance when our daily life is so ordinary, hidden and humble. The thirty hidden years of Jesus the first Son can surely help us to take this revelation about ourselves more seriously and to find a new and deep joy in our own being.

The Psalmist reminds us that we are not our own makers, that we have been created in love by our Father, God. Paul tells us we have been recreated by Jesus who gave his life's blood to seal his love for us. He writes to the Corinthians, 'You are not your own property; you have been bought and paid for' (I Co 6:20). I believe much of life's fear, suffering and anxiety comes from not recognising and joyfully accepting the amazing wonder and truth of our divine connection. We want to live as if we were our own creators, as if we were our own property.

Listen to a story. A man was walking along a country road into town one morning. On the way he met another man coming from the market leading a heavily laden donkey. The load was so heavy the poor animal staggered and fell, whereupon the owner beat the donkey till it struggled to its feet. The other man was upset by this and began to scold the owner of the donkey for his cruelty, only to receive the angry reply, 'Mind your own business. This is my donkey and I will do what I like with my own property.' The man listened, thought for a while and then suddenly began to beat the owner of the donkey with the walking stick he carried. When the donkey's owner began to curse and berate him, he answered simply, 'Mind your own business. This is my walking stick and I do what I like with my own property!' I think we can easily find ourselves saying to God, 'This is my life and I do what I like with my own property.' The great Buddha laughs at those who speak this way. He mocks those who say, this is mine, that is mine, and comments, 'These are the words of a fool who does not understand that even he is not his.'

If we insist that our lives are our own and deny our origin, then we cut ourselves off from our ultimate roots and cut ourselves off from true life. We cannot grow as we should nor find our true fulfilment. Our fear, of course, is that if we admit that our origin is from another, that we are not our own property, then we may lose our freedom, our personal independence. We want to be our own person and decide our own destiny. These are understandable sentiments and express a universal wish of the human spirit. Psychologists tell us that we must own our own self in the sense of not allowing a domineering other person, maybe a parent or teacher, to shape and control our inner world. But God our Father created us precisely to be our own unique selves and he has the greatest respect for our freedom. I believe that there is no real conflict or problem here once we understand the fullness of the Good News that Jesus brought, namely that the God who is our origin is Love.

Jesus invites us to surrender to God as to a lover. Surrender can have two very different meanings depending on the context. There is a surrender that is imposed on me when I am forced to submit to a stronger power that defeats me. This kind of surrender humiliates me, takes away my freedom and destroys my self-respect. But there is another surrender that I freely make. This is the surrender that lovers experience when they discover another who is good and beautiful and who sees them in the same light and wants to share all with them. The whole desire now is to surrender to this other and this kind of surrender is not seen as servitude or burden but brings joy, elation and deepest fulfilment.

Jesus saw God in this light and joyfully surrendered to his Father's love. He invites us to see God in this way and to surrender ourselves to his love. Then comes the wonderful discovery that this surrender brings the possibility of the most authentic fulfilment of self. Not only do we not lose ourselves in such surrender, but we even find our own true selves, or perhaps more accurately, we have the beautiful experience of being found by the other, by love. It is only when we allow ourselves to be found and possessed by love that we will discover that we can possess everything. I believe that this was the experience of Jesus which he wanted to share with us.

4

OUR TRUE IDENTITY

The teaching and life of Jesus were motivated by one supreme value, love. For him love was the only absolute – love of God and of one another. This was not some sudden insight that struck him. This conviction was the fruit of his hidden years. Again we ask what Jesus did during the long years of his hidden life. We have said he did none of the things we would have expected him to do in preparation for the task ahead. St Luke says simply, 'Jesus increased in wisdom, in stature and in favour with God and men' (Lk 2:52). So Jesus is doing nothing in the sense of achieving but he is growing, becoming more and more his hidden true self. Much of that growth must have gone on in that hidden place we call prayer. We know that later in his busy public life he will often slip away on his own to be in prayer with his Father. Such prayer must surely have been his most significant activity in the hidden life. There he grows in awareness of his identity as the beloved Son, like a young prince growing in the realisation of what it means to be the son of the King. He grows in the certainty that the Father is love and that he loves each person with unconditional love. In prayer he learns all those secrets of his Father which he will gladly share with us in his later teaching.

In prayer, Jesus sends down deep roots into the nourishing soil of his Father's love. His life is planted in love. These roots will have to go deep and be firm for the tree to stand up to the storm that will later shake and batter it to try and uproot it. He will be tested to the full in his love for his Father and for us. The supreme test will come when he is asked to let go his young life in death, in the certainty that love is stronger than death. Being human like us, his spirit is revolted at the prospect of undeserved suffering and early death and in the garden of Gethsemane he asks his Father to save him from this fate. But he is committed with the Father to love and if this is what love asks, he will go through with it. So when his captors come to take him, he is calm and strong and he lets them know he has not been deserted by his Father. 'Do you think that I cannot appeal to my Father who would promptly send more than twelve legions of angels to my defence?' (Mt 26:53).

It is in silent prayer with his Father that he grows in wisdom.

Here, through long silent years, he prepares for that speech which will later amaze his listeners. A modern poet, speaking of the poetic art, reflects on the place of silence in the poet's life. He writes, 'Before we can ever say anything, anything at all, we must link ourselves by a long silent process to the Reality. Only long hours of silence can lead us to our language.' The Reality Jesus explores is the inner being and mystery of God which he will later reveal to us. He did not think that thirty years of silence was too long for him to link himself with this Reality. This silent prayer leads him to his language and we should not wonder that later on people will say, 'There has never been anyone who has spoken like this man.' Out of this silent communing with the Father will come the story of the Prodigal Son. There Jesus will give us the inside story of the heart of our Father God. The words he puts into the mouth of the Father in that story are the words given to him by that same Father. 'What the Father has told me is what I speak' (Jn 12:50). So when the father in that story says to his elder son, 'My son, you are with me always and all I have is yours', Jesus says these words with total conviction and the listeners know that they are true and that God really wants to share everything with them. Their hearts are convinced. They share in Jesus' own joy in the Father. This is what they meant when they said, 'He speaks with authority' (Mk 1:22).

Jesus rejoices to share the mystery of God's love with simple hidden people. We need not envy those people. The living Lord through all time continues to reveal these life-giving secrets to those who will listen in prayer. We too are invited to experience that other hidden life we call prayer. At the Last Supper Jesus speaks not only to his apostles but to all of us when he says, 'I call you friends, because I have made known to you everything I have learnt from my Father' (Jn 15:15). And this experience of sharing his Father's love with us is for him a most joyful experience. 'It was then that, filled with joy by the Holy Spirit, he said, "I bless you, Father, Lord of heaven and of earth, for hiding these things from the learned and the clever and revealing them to mere children. Yes, Father, for that is what it pleased you to do. Everything has been entrusted to me by my Father; and no one knows who the son is except the Father, and who the Father is except the Son and those to whom the Son chooses to reveal him"' (Lk 10:21-22). Jesus rejoices to be with us, his friends, in prayer so that he can share the inner secrets of God, just as anyone would look forward joyfully to an intimate chat with a dear friend. He joins us in prayer rejoicing. What a pity we often look on prayer as a duty, as something we must do to win God's favour.

How kind of Jesus to describe prayer as a meeting of friends! Most people would agree that their life assumes meaning and value not so much from the possessions they have as from their friends. A true friend is a rare possession and treasure. Will my life not become more meaningful and worthwhile when I realise that Jesus calls me friend and that that friendship can deepen and grow as the years pass? A friend is one we share secrets with, one we go to with sorrows, problems, failure. The company of a friend is a kind of resting place where I can be renewed. Recently I received from a friend a postcard which showed a scenic little village on the north coast of Ireland. The few houses were close to a quiet beach and protecting mountains towered up behind the village. The scene was the epitome of peace and rest. My friend had been under a lot of pressure from tension and overwork. She went to this village to unwind, to recover balance, peace and energy so as to be able to go on living more humanly and peacefully. Thinking of the beauty, peace and rest suggested by this postcard, I suddenly saw it as an image of friendship and prayer. Is a friend not such a resting place, a place that accepts me, just as the mountains and the sea accept me as I am, with no trace of judgement? A quiet retreat and a friend both invite me to relax, to shed care, to rediscover meaning, to identify true values and to believe that I am loved. And does our friend Jesus not say, 'Come to me, all you who labour and are overburdened, and I will give you rest' (Mt 11:28)?

A friend is one who knows all about you and still loves you. I suppose one of the deepest desires we all have is to be fully known by another and still be accepted. We feel we do not want to get love and approval under false pretences. We would like to reveal the very worst about ourselves, but in that same moment we are afraid that if the worst were known, we might be rejected. A true friend can be our salvation here. When we make a foolish mistake or give in deliberately to some sin, we are blessed if we have a friend to whom we can reveal this meanness and ugliness. I speak of more than confessing and receiving forgiveness in the Sacrament of Reconciliation. I speak of personal acceptance by another person. Perhaps I go to this friend and say, 'I am so disappointed with myself. I have done something of which I am very ashamed. I am a really bad person.' A true friend will listen and say, 'No, you

22

are not a bad person. Yes, you have done a bad thing. We all do sometimes. You admit the evil and renounce it, but you are good and lovable to God and to me.' A true friend must say something like that. Jesus calls us friends. He is such a friend. He will not only reveal God to us in prayer, but will reveal our own better selves as well. Jesus knows the worst and still accepts and loves us.

A true friend should keep me in touch with deeper reality and keep alive in me a sense of meaning in life, a sense of my own true value. Jesus our friend does this when we meet in prayer. Notice that in these pages we speak of the hidden life of Jesus and of our own hidden life. We do not speak of hidden 'existence'. Life suggests more than existence. It suggests meaning, purpose, value and growth. We should aim to be fully alive and not just to exist. We can exist without prayer. But we cannot live without it. Life does not remain static, nor does friendship. They either grow and blossom or they wither and die. The Lord calls us friends and wants the friendship to grow and be fruitful in our lives. This cannot happen without prayer. How can I love someone I don't know? How can I know someone I don't meet? And how can I meet Jesus if I don't pray? One of his own images of prayer is the relationship of branch and tree. 'A branch cannot bear fruit all by itself, but must remain part of the vine' (Jn 15:4). As Jesus in his prayer life grew into deep awareness of his true identity as the beloved Son of God, so in our prayer life we too will be led deeper into the mystery of our own being and the wonder of our true identity as the beloved of God. Many of our fears and problems in life are related to a false perception of who we really are.

A story may help us here. A psychiatrist welcomes a new client and asks about his problem. The client, obviously very disturbed, says he is very upset about his troops in Russia! When the psychiatrist asks him to explain, the client says he ordered his troops to invade Russia but now winter has come and he fears his troops will be cut off and massacred. The psychiatrist politely asks, 'I don't think you gave me your name. Who are you?' The client answers, 'I am Napoleon Bonaparte and my problem is how to rescue my troops from Russia. Can you help me?' Clearly this poor man's problem arises from the sad confusion over his identity. The psychiatrist's job will not be to offer advice on how to rescue the troops, but how to help the man to solve his identity crisis. As soon as the man is convinced he is not Napoleon he won't be worried

23

about his troops! When he reaches that understanding, his problem will have disappeared.

If only we could shake off that false identity which tells us that we are on our own in coping with life's problems and that God is even part of the problem. If we could shed that false identity and know who we truly are, the children of God and friends of Jesus, and know that our God is one hundred per cent on our side, then many fears would vanish and many problems would lose their power to frighten and oppress us.

5

Holy Family.

VISIONS BUT NO PILGRIMS

Jesus had two close and beloved companions all through the hidden years in Nazareth: Joseph and Mary. Their names would mean nothing outside that small country village, but further on, in a place called heaven, they would be the focus of immense respect and affection. And two thousand years later, many children in many lands will be named after them. Surely St Paul's words apply with particular force to them. 'The life you have is hidden with Christ in God' (Col 3:3).

Joseph is an unknown village carpenter but he still has heavenly visitors. These visits did not make headlines in any Nazareth newspaper. No local religious leader, no parish priest gets wind of strange happenings. No reports reach any higher religious authority. No bishop is called in to pronounce on the event. Nazareth is not invaded by pilgrims. The secret plans of God which will affect the future of all creation are being revealed to a young engaged couple, but all is quiet in Nazareth. Joseph is told that the young woman he is in love with and hopes to marry is very close to God and highly favoured. She will be the mother of the Messiah and Joseph must not fear to take her home as his wife (Mt 1:20). This young village carpenter has a new role assigned to him which places him at the heart of God's plan of salvation, but this role will not be played out on the stage of any great capital city. It will be a hidden role in this quiet village.

A hidden role does not mean an easy role. Joseph is made privy to God's inner secrets and plans but this brings no privileges of the kind we would expect. Indeed Joseph quickly discovers that to be called close to God can turn life upside down, involve danger and demand great sacrifice. Soon after the birth of this special child whom he has been chosen to rear and protect, unexpected danger threatens. The danger comes from the palace of the King. Now, King Herod does not lead a hidden life. He is much in the public eye. His life of luxury, lust and cruelty is public knowledge. He hears rumours of the birth of a possible rival. Herod knows only one kind of king, the kind who might challenge his power. How could he know that this new king would want people's hearts rather than their taxes or their lands? Joseph has to flee to

25

protect his wife and young son. This holy family joins the thousands of hidden families who have to run away from tyranny. We see them night after night on our TV screens, those streams of hopeless, homeless people clogging the roads and bush paths and mountain passes of different lands, worried, helpless fathers, distraught mothers clutching their babies. As we watch them, feeling so helpless ourselves, let us be sure that their lives too are hidden with Christ in God and that their names are all written in heaven.

Eventually the family is able to return. They settle in Nazareth and Joseph continues his life as a carpenter. He is known in the village community, but only as the carpenter. No one can later recall anything strange or unusual about him when his son begins to attract attention and excite wonder. The words of surprise provoked by the wisdom and miracles of Jesus tell us what people knew and thought of Joseph. 'This is the carpenter's son, surely?' (Mt 13:55). He is the carpenter and he will be joined in that trade by the young lad who played around the shop in his early years. Father and son must have worked together for a number of years. We presume Joseph died before Jesus left Nazareth, but we do not know. This great and much-loved saint ends a hidden life with a hidden death.

We think of Jesus' other companion, his mother Mary. As a young girl she was indistinguishable from the other girls in the village. She was unknown to the world of her day, but she is loved by millions in our day. She may have been an ordinary girl in the eyes of the village but in God's eyes she is very special. One day God sends his messenger Gabriel to this girl. The angel greets her as highly favoured by God and invites her to rejoice. In fact Mary does not rejoice but is filled with confusion. Then, to this girl so young and so hidden, is revealed God's intended fulfilment of that prophecy which had kept the hopes and dreams of her people alive through many centuries, the coming of the Messiah. When she discovers later that Joseph too knows the secret, she could say to him what Paul later applies to us all: 'God has let us know the mystery of his purpose, the hidden plan he so kindly made in Christ from the beginning' (Ep 1:9).

St Luke concludes his description of the meeting between angel and maiden with these words, '"I am the handmaid of the Lord", said Mary, "let what you have said be done to me." And the angel left her' (Lk 1:38). What an anti-climax. 'And the angel left her.' I wonder did Mary go to the door of her home and look out on to the quiet village street? Did she expect to see some sign of the incredible drama which had just been inaugurated? But all is quiet. Nazareth has noticed nothing. The great world of empire, politics, conquest and trade rolls on unaware of this obscure village and this hidden girl. But the seed of love has been sown in a heart ready to receive it and it will grow in the dark as seeds do. Later there will be a village wedding. God will be the chief guest but no one will notice.

Mary grew as her son grew in favour with God, and people and prayer must have played a great part in that growth process. We are told that 'Mary treasured all these things and pondered them in her heart' (Lk 2:20). Notice that Mary 'treasured' all these things. This young woman has the right sense of values. This deep and hidden reality which is being revealed is 'treasure' to her. Mary knows what is precious and valuable. This revelation tells her that God has remembered his promises, that he cares and comes to his people whom he loves. This is treasure. What is the wealth of a Herod or a Caesar compared to this? This treasure of God's love will be offered to all people and all can have their lives transformed when they discover it. In fairy stories treasure is often buried on remote mysterious islands or deep in castle dungeons. But this treasure revealed now to our hearts is in fact hidden close at land, indeed within our hearts. Mary's son will assure us of this later, telling us that 'the kingdom of God is within you'.

When will this son begin to speak these and other words of good news to us? When will the seed grow and bear fruit? When will that which is now hidden be shouted from the housetops? Surely the light has not been brought into the room of this world to be hidden under a bushel. Mary does not know. Joseph does not know. They must wait for God. They believe, trust and wait. God's timing is always best. This waiting is not an empty time. It is not an absence of doing or achieving. It is a way of being. 'It is good to wait in silence for Yahweh to save' (Lm 3:26). This is true greatness in God's sight.

One day, years later, when Jesus is teaching, a woman in the crowd will cry out spontaneously in praise of Mary: 'Happy the womb that bore you and the breast you sucked' (Lk 11:27). Jesus in his reply seems to make little of this gracious compliment. 'But he replied, "Still happier those who hear the word of God and keep it"' (Lk 11:28). Jesus here is not refusing the praise offered to his mother but is drawing our attention to her true greatness. This greatness, in his eyes, lies not so much in her physical maternity but in her total trust of God's message brought by the angel. The 'word' Jesus speaks of here is not any commandment, but God's word of love. Mary heard it, believed and trusted God. 'Be it done unto me according to your word.' Her greatness lay not in the externals of being his physical mother, but in that more hidden greatness of her complete trust in God's word all through those long years in Nazareth when nothing seemed to be happening. Jesus does not want us to miss the true greatness of his mother. And that kind of greatness lies within our power. It is good to trust Yahweh and to wait in silence for him to save us. Mary will be glad to help us.

6

THEY DID NOT UNDERSTAND

During those long years of waiting in Nazareth, Mary and Joseph must often have talked together about their son. They would recall the words of the heavenly messengers, 'He is the one who is to save his people from their sins' (Mt 1:21); and, 'He will be great. The Lord God will give him the throne of his ancestor David' (Lk 1:32). No explanations were given to this young married couple, no programme as to when or how these prophecies would be fulfilled. They were simply invited to believe, to trust and to wait on God. When, at the age of twelve, their son was lost on a pilgrimage to Jerusalem, we are told of their great anxiety as parents. When they find him they express their concern at his behaviour. When Jesus answers and speaks of a great hidden force in his life, his heavenly Father's work, we are told simply that the parents did not understand. 'They did not understand what he meant' (Lk 2:50). If God's plan unfolds in such a slow and hidden way for these two great friends of his, can we not be more patient and believe that in our own lives, with their ordinary problems, cares and many unanswered questions, God is present, at work, and knows what he is doing?

Mary and Joseph must often have wondered when their son would begin his great saving task. But in fact for him it had already begun. For him the task always is to do his Father's will; right now his Father is asking him to identify with the world of ordinary folk and, by so doing, lead them to see that no life is just ordinary. The life of each person is extraordinary, full of wonder because of God's love. The gaze of God's love rests on each person as it did through those hidden years on that young carpenter in Nazareth, his beloved Son. God is asking us through Jesus to question our assumptions about what is important in life. He invites us to go below the surface of our 'ordinary' daily life and rejoice in the wonder and beauty of God present to us in love.

Jesus is not just putting in time in Nazareth, waiting to begin his saving work. There is a very hidden preparation going on as he grows in intimacy with his Father. He is entering into the total certainty that his Father is love and that that love embraces not only himself but all of his Father's creation. He has come to build a kingdom of love, healing and justice. Later he will speak in parable about building and say that a careful builder will check that he has all the materials before he starts to build. 'Which of you here, intending to build a tower, would not first sit down and work out the cost to see if he had enough to complete it? Otherwise, if he had laid the foundation and then found himself unable to finish the work, the onlookers would all start making fun of him and saying, "Here is a man who started to build and was unable to finish"' (Lk 14:28-30). Jesus has come to build not a tower but the kingdom of God. He will do this no matter what the cost because he is in love with God and with all of us. Part of the cost is this long, hidden life.

In another parable, Jesus says it would be a foolish king who would challenge another king to battle without first checking out his weapons and the strength of his army. 'What king marching to war against another king would not first sit down and consider whether with ten thousand men he could stand up to the other who advanced against him with twenty thousand?' (Lk 14:31). Jesus will be advancing against the oldest enemy of humankind, the Prince of this world, who marshals his weapons of fear, greed, hate, pride and ultimately death itself. It is a fearsome army to face. It will surely be a terrible war, but when the last battle is fought on a hill called Calvary, the victory will be with this young carpenter, our champion, who will rely on one weapon only, love. During the hidden years in Nazareth that love will become so strong and powerful that no evil force will ever be able to overcome it.

But just now there are no signs of the coming battle. There is a quiet village and a hidden family. I believe that it is not only Mary and Joseph who wait and wonder when their son is to move out into a more public life and activity. I think that Jesus too waits on his Father's will and wonders. He is now thirty years of age. How will he know when he should leave Nazareth and move into a public ministry? We are not told of any dramatic happening. It seems that there were no heavenly messengers like those who came to Mary and Joseph at the beginning of the story. I suspect that the signal came to Jesus in the most ordinary and unobtrusive way.

I imagine Mary going to the well one morning. As she draws water from the well, she overhears conversation from an excited group of women. One of the women of the village has just returned from visiting friends in Jerusalem. She is sharing the latest news from the big city. She says there is much talk about strange happenings at the river Jordan. An exciting new prophet has appeared from the solitude of the desert and is drawing large crowds with his charismatic preaching and his offer of a baptism of repentance. He is called John and is making the startling claim that the Messiah is about to appear in the land. Mary has just lifted the bucket from the well when she hears these last words. Her heart misses a beat. The bucket tumbles back into the well. Her neighbours look at her and ask if she is all right. Back at the house she composes herself and then goes down to the shop to ask her son if he has heard the news.

Or maybe Jesus hears the news first. He is working in the shop when a horse pulls up outside. The rider comes in and asks if Jesus can do a repair job on his saddle. Jesus gets some tools and begins to work and they chat. The man talks about his travels and an interesting experience he had last week. Up in Jerusalem he had heard that a new prophet had appeared at the Jordan and was moving the hearts of many people. Since his journey home brought him near this new place of pilgrimage, he decided to go down to the river. When Jesus asked what it was like, the man said that the new prophet, called John, was certainly a powerful preacher. 'Did you say his name was John?' Jesus stops his work and asks. 'Yes, he is called John, but when he was asked who he was, he did not use the name John. He said he was just a voice sent to prepare the way for one much greater than himself.' Jesus is very still now. The man continues, 'I was very impressed by John but could not be sure how balanced he might be! He said one thing which made me doubt. After saying he was preparing the way, he then said that in fact the Messiah was standing among us, only we could not recognise him. Well, I ask you, carpenter, can you imagine how you could be standing beside the Messiah and not recognise him? Anyway, thanks for the job and if you have a few free days you should go over to the Jordan and see and hear John for yourself. Goodbye and shalom.' The man leaves the shop. Horse and rider gallop off and silence returns to the street. Jesus says to himself, 'Yes, I think I should go over to the Jordan.' He locks up shop for a while and goes home to ask Mary if she has heard the news.

So the waiting and preparation are over. The time has come. In some such simple and unobtrusive way God gives the signal to his

31

beloved Son. No heavenly messenger, no thunder or flash of lightning; no fanfare as our young champion leaves Nazareth to go forth and challenge the ancient enemy of all humankind on our behalf.

7

BRIDGE OVER TROUBLED WATERS

And so Jesus goes to the Jordan. The hidden life is over. As he enters his public ministry we expect drama, action and publicity. But, as always, we have it wrong. Our ways are never his. 'Yes, the heavens are as high above earth as my ways are above your ways, my thoughts above your thoughts' (Is 55:9). A great crowd has gathered at the Jordan. Their hearts have been prepared by John's charismatic preaching. There is an excited air of expectancy. It's a fitting stage for the inauguration of the Kingdom. We would expect Jesus to consult with John and invite the prophet to introduce him to the multitude. This would give credence to John's prophecy and would be a dramatic launching of the Messiah's mission. Then Jesus could take over and begin preaching and baptising. How totally different is the reality. Jesus may have left the quiet village of Nazareth and moved into the midst of a great throng of noisy, excited, expectant people, but he is still opting for a very hidden role. He does not separate himself from the crowd but mixes with them. He sits at their camp fires, shares their food, listens with them to John's preaching and then joins them as they make their way to the river. There he wades through the shallow water with them to ask for baptism.

What is going on here? Will we ever be able even to begin to understand the ways of God? Remember this man's name is Jesus, which means 'the one who will save his people from their sins'. The name was chosen in heaven because of its meaning. In Zambian society the family carefully chooses the name for the newborn child. The name is significant. It has special meaning and tells us something about the child. The work of this young man, his mission in the world, is of such great significance that God chooses the name. It is not left to the earthly parents. God is taking no chances. He is making sure we will understand well the meaning of Jesus and why he has come. The angel said to Joseph, 'Mary will give birth to a son and you must name him Jesus, because he is the one who is to save his people from their sins' (Mt 1:21).

Note that his work is to save. He comes not to judge or condemn his people but to save them. Now at the Jordan we begin to see how he is going to do that saving work. He will do it in a way so wonderful and beautiful that only God could have thought of it. He will save us from our sins, not by separating himself from us or judging us, but by identifying with us, by coming so close to us in our sin and brokenness that he will take away our fear and shame and release great new healing energy in our hearts. How can we fear someone who stands beside us for baptism? How can we be ashamed in the presence of a God who rubs shoulders with us as we confess our failure and our need for help in the River Jordan? What a hidden God and how beautiful his ways.

The lives of most people are very hidden. They do not make the headlines. Most of us remain unknown outside a small circle of family and friends. We are not people of wealth or influence in society and we are not celebrated for any achievement. Jesus asks us to look beyond all these externals. He invites us to search deeper in the heart for the true value and beauty deep within us. But this can bring a new problem. People are afraid to make this inner journey because they fear facing their inner selves. They prefer to live on the surface of life, believing that if they look too deeply within themselves they will find only failure, weakness and sin. When Jesus stood in the queue of sinners in the Jordan, he was saying to us, 'I know you have that problem. I know about all that interior mess but I still love you and want you to believe that that is not your real self. You must go deeper still. I have come to escort you past the mess to your true self.' St Augustine, talking of this inner journey, says, 'I entered into my own depths with you as my guide.' If we make this journey alone we can be very discouraged. But if Jesus is our guide he will lift us and carry us over the muddy patches to that true centre where God stays and delights to be. That queue in the River Jordan is found in every age and culture. No man or woman can say, 'I don't belong there.' That's why Jesus did not stay on the Jordan bank but got right down into that line of people to save and rescue them and us from fear, guilt and self-hatred by his gentleness and loving acceptance of us in all our brokenness.

This loving acceptance of us as we are can be the start of healing and a new and more joyful life. Jesus is as close to us and as accepting of us as he was to those people in the Jordan. He has not come to call the successful but the failures. Even more, he has come to tell us that in his eyes there are no failures. He does not use that language. Some extraordinary healing power is released when we realise that we are totally accepted by God who is Love and by Jesus who is that Love made visible. One of the most destructive effects of personal sin and failure is the loss of self-esteem, leading to self-hatred and the fear of trying again. Jesus wants to save us from all this. True love never makes the other person feel insignificant or a failure. It does not generate fear or guilt but, rather, a healing process. Some years ago in a TV documentary on Taizé, one young man, when asked what was his deepest impression of the place, answered, 'This is one sacred place I have come to where I know I am in a sacred place and yet I don't feel guilty.' Those who were close to Jesus must have had some similar experience. I think of Chesterton's definition of a saint: 'a sinner who knows he or she is forgiven'. Because of Jesus we can apply Paul's words with new force to the discouraged sinner: 'The life you have is hidden with Christ in God.'

Sometimes our weakness and sin do not remain hidden but receive unwelcome publicity. Sadly it can happen that those whose lives are otherwise quite hidden may suddenly find themselves thrust into the public eye because of some failure or weakness that becomes a public scandal and the subject of common gossip. Someone is exposed for cheating in a public exam, a marriage breaks down and ends in the divorce courts, a son is discovered to be taking drugs, a priest is dying of AIDS, a quiet young girl becomes pregnant outside marriage, a woman's secret drinking habit is publicised. The list is as long as that queue in the Jordan. Again Jesus stands with us to help us cope with the humiliation that comes from such an experience. In a special way he wants to draw our attention to our deeper goodness and beauty which is temporarily obscured by notoriety, ugly publicity and gossip. He is nearby to help us to recover our faith in our own deep, true, good selves.

One day early in his public life Jesus waits at a wayside well for a woman in this predicament. She is a Samaritan woman from a small nearby town, a quiet place like his own Nazareth. She is a hidden woman but her failure is not hidden. The townsfolk know of her sins, her many affairs and her present immoral union. They will remind her of her failure and confirm her in her poor image of herself. She goes out to the well alone. Jesus looks at life and people quite differently. It makes no difference to him that she has a bad name, nor, as we would say, that she is not a member of his Church! What matters is that she needs love and healing. This man

35

looks with eyes of love which always see the hidden beauty and goodness which other eyes fail to see. Slow, patient, gentle loving is needed to get past the layers of public condemnation, humiliation and self-hatred to the deeper goodness and beauty. Only love can ease away the fears and self-condemnation of the sinner and create an atmosphere for healing. Maybe this woman does not know that his name is Jesus, but that day she experiences his saving power and her step is light as she hurries back to the town, no longer ashamed or afraid, to call out the neighbours to meet this man. The meeting with this woman was possible because Jesus' own glory and divinity are hidden in his humanity. This humanity is God's bridge over the troubled waters of sin and failure, the bridge that brings him right into our troubled hearts.

8

THE 'BEST MAN' FOR JESUS

Before we leave the Jordan and follow Jesus into his public ministry, let us pause and look at this prophet who has come from the desert and is drawing crowds with his preaching. This intriguing man is another hidden person like Joseph, Mary and Jesus himself. His story invites us again to look for real greatness, not on the surface of life but in its more hidden places. John is about thirty years of age when he emerges from the desert and appears at the Jordan. His birth was surrounded by signs and wonders. Then he disappeared for thirty years. For a short time he took centre stage at the Jordan. 'All Judaea and all the people of Jerusalem made their way to him' (Mk 1:5) Then he dares to challenge King Herod about his immoral life. Queen Herodias is angry and has him imprisoned. So John returns to another chapter of hidden life in a dungeon in Herod's palace. Then one night there is a wild birthday party for the King. The noise of the palace revelry reaches John in his dungeon below. Next he hears footsteps approach the cell. The King's attendants enter. One bears a large dish but it does not carry a slice of the birthday cake! The King's executioner pulls out his sword and does his job. John is beheaded and his head is brought on the dish to satisfy Queen Herodias. So ends the life of John. If we were searching for true greatness that night in Herod's palace, would we seek to interview the King in his banquet hall upstairs or go below to the dungeons to talk to John?

Let us go back to the circumstances of his birth. It was a time of great expectations. His father Zachary had a vision in the Temple telling him that his wife Elizabeth, though advanced in years, would bear a son. 'You must name him John. Many will rejoice at his birth, for he will be great in the sight of the Lord' (Lk:13-14). When Zachary doubts the heavenly messenger he is struck dumb. Elizabeth conceives and gives birth to a baby boy. On the eighth day all gather for the ceremony of circumcision and naming. Relatives want to name him Zachary after his father but Elizabeth says no, the name must be John. Zachary is consulted. 'The father asked for a writing tablet and wrote, "His name is John." And they were all astonished. At that instant his power of speech returned and he spoke and praised God. All their neighbours were filled with awe and the whole affair was talked about throughout the hill country of Judaea. "What will this child turn out to be?" they wondered' (Lk 1:63-66).

'What will this child turn out to be?' Surely this thought must echo in the hearts of all parents. Every birth invites us to wonder at the gift and mystery of each new life and all parents surely dream dreams for their children. Given the unusual circumstances of this child's birth, we are not surprised that relatives and friends expected a special and wonderful future for him. We can imagine their expectations. Surely this child will be famous, will do wonderful deeds and make a great name in history. But things often do not turn out the way we expect. As with Jesus after his birth, a great veil falls over the story of this child. We will not hear of him again till he appears at the Jordan. St Luke summarises the intervening thirty years with these words: 'Meanwhile the child grew up and his spirit matured. And he lived out in the wilderness until the day he appeared openly to Israel' (Lk 1:80). So while Jesus the Messiah hides in the obscurity of Nazareth, John his herald is hidden in the wilderness. Maybe he lives a hermit's life or joins a desert community. We are not told. But we can be sure that during those years, in hidden prayer, John must have explored the mystery he is to speak of. Those long years of silence lead this man who calls himself a voice to the language that will fire the hearts of those who flock to the Jordan. St Luke says that in those years 'his spirit matured'. It is a long slow growth for a very brief flowering. But, in God's eyes, greatness is not measured in time.

When John does appear and begins his mission of preparing people's hearts for the Messiah, we see that he has learned well. He seeks no greatness or praise for himself. He is not founding a church or a religion. He does not try to build up a personal cult or attract a following for himself. John is totally Jesus-centred. He has left the hidden life of the desert, but not to seek personal glory or popularity. The deepest current of his own personal life is still hidden. All his great prophetic energy, all his powerful preaching is directed to one end only, to introduce and reveal the Messiah. The curious Jordan pilgrims ask, 'Who are you? What have you to say about yourself?' (Jn 1:22-23). John answers, 'I am a voice that cries in the wilderness, "Make a straight way for the Lord"' (Jn 1:23). In the presence of this Lord he is introducing, he feels totally unworthy, 'not fit to kneel down and undo the strap of his sandals' (Mk 1:7). Such a preacher must attract devoted disciples. So it happens, but when Jesus appears, John will encourage those disciples to leave him and go with Jesus, saying, 'He must grow greater, I must grow smaller' (Jn 3:30).

John sees his meaning and identity as intimately linked with those of Jesus. He is a totally unselfish person. Indeed, John is so austerely single-minded that he can overawe us, even frighten us. But in one place, he gives us a glimpse of a softer and warmer part of himself. Speaking about his relationship with Jesus, he says, 'The bride is only for the bridegroom; and yet the bridegroom's friend, who stands there and listens, is glad when he hears the bridegroom's voice. This same joy I feel, and now it is complete' (Jn 3:29). Thus John describes Jesus as the bridegroom. This image, which pictures God's people as a bride being courted by a loving God, was used by earlier prophets. We might not have expected it from this austere prophet. Yet here it is with an added warm touch where John describes himself as the friend of Christ, the bridegroom. John is the best man whose whole joy is to work for the success of this love covenant between God and us.

We can say that John's greatness lay in his genuine humility and total lack of any self-interest. Let us consider an even deeper level of greatness in this man, where, paradoxically, he may come closer to you and me in our hidden lives of faith. John's whole purpose and meaning in life was to introduce the Messiah to Israel. Yet when Jesus the Messiah comes to the Jordan, he turns John's world upside down by asking to be baptised. Thus Jesus upsets all John's expectations and the prophet expresses his confusion, 'John tried to dissuade him. "It is I who need baptism from you", he said, "and yet you come to me!"' But Jesus replied, "Leave it like this for the time being; it is fitting that we should, in this way, do all that righteousness demands." At this, John gave in to him' (Mt 3:14-15).

So we have John chosen by God to play a key role in his great plan of salvation, without understanding God's ways. Surely this is real greatness, which was also the greatness of Mary and Joseph and even Jesus. They all walked in total trust that God was in charge and knew what he was doing even when they did not understand. I think we do a great injustice to the saints and to their true greatness and holiness by imagining that it was easy for them because they must have understood God's plans. We imagine that they knew the inside story and were spared doubts and questioning. It was not so. Their true greatness lay in trusting God completely even when things did not go as they had hoped or expected. They persevered despite darkness and uncertainty. We can be like them in this. But because this is a tough kind of holiness, we try to excuse ourselves by suggesting that it was different for the saints.

The last recorded incident in John's story before his death emphasises this aspect of his greatness. From his prison cell in Herod's dungeons, John follows with interest the activities of Jesus the Messiah. The news he receives is, again, not what he expected. Jesus did not stay at the Jordan baptising. He does not seem so concerned about an imminent judgement on sin and evil. He is moving about healing the sick, even on the Sabbath, and fraternising with sinners. John is so disturbed, he begins to doubt. St Luke reports, 'The disciples of John gave him all this news, and John, summoning two of his disciples, sent them to the Lord to ask, "Are you the one who is to come, or must we wait for someone else?"' (Lk 7:18-19). What a poignant question! 'Are you the one who is to come?' This word questions not only the identity of Jesus, but even that of John himself. John described himself as the voice introducing the Messiah. If Jesus is not the Messiah, then where does that leave John? This must have been a self-emptying which even John would not have expected. John is not destined to taste the sweetness of success or achievement, as indeed, neither will his dear bridegroom, the Messiah. In our worldly judgement both John and Jesus are colossal failures. In the Mass of the Feast of John the Baptist one of the scripture readings from Isaiah is beautifully appropriate. Isaiah prophesies about the suffering of the expected Messiah. How well the prophecy applies also to John his herald. 'He said to me, "You are my servant Israel in whom I shall be glorified", while I was thinking, "I have toiled in vain, I have exhausted myself for nothing"' (Is 49:3-4). It must have seemed to John in his dungeon, as it did to Jesus later on the cross, that he had laboured in vain and exhausted himself for nothing. But then Isaiah the prophet continues and leads us into that deeper hidden reality that applies to John, to Jesus, to you and me and all who try to trust in the Lord:

> And all the while my cause was with Yahweh, my
> reward with my God. I was honoured in the eyes of
> Yahweh, my God was my strength.
>
> Isaiah 49:4-5

Let the last word on John come from Jesus. 'When John's messengers had gone, Jesus began to talk to the people about John. "I tell you, of all the children born of women, there is no one greater than John"' (Lk 7:24-28). We have been exploring John's greatness and have noted as one of its highest points that John kept going even when he did not understand God's ways. We can be like him in this. We can sometimes feel that our faith life is all in vain, but if we just try to keep going, we too shall experience God as our strength.

9

THE GAUNTLET IS PICKED UP

As we look at Jesus and observe his choices, his lifestyle and his teaching, we are looking at God's clearest revelation of himself. The hidden life of Nazareth was a deliberate choice. The first act of his public life was another amazing choice, to join sinners in the Jordan and ask for baptism. These choices are related to his own deepest meaning and purpose, which is to reveal God, his Father and our Father, to the world. These choices challenge our traditional ideas about God and how he relates to us. We need not be ashamed if we have to admit that we do not understand God and his ways. Mary did not understand and John the Baptist was shocked and even wondered if Jesus was the Messiah. But let us be open to learning from Jesus about God and about ourselves and about the rich meaning of our lives. By wading into the Jordan waters and asking for baptism, Jesus reveals a strategy for salvation which should fill us with wonder and joy. He is saying he has not come to impose salvation on us, to manipulate us through threats and fear or to bribe us with heavenly rewards. He has come to get close, very close to us in our hurts and our failures and thus to assure us that he understands our human predicament and offers a loving companionship powerful enough to heal and renew us.

How could Jesus be so sure of himself and his decision to ask for baptism in the Jordan? How could he so confidently break with the traditional ideas of God and of his attitude to sin? John is shocked. The scribes, Pharisees and all the other self-righteous people are scandalised. Only sinners appreciate and experience this as the beginning of salvation. By this gesture Jesus steps on to a path which will eventually lead to Calvary. How could he be so sure that he was on the right path? Because he was sure it was his Father's way. And he was sure of this because he spent much time with his Father in prayer. At the moment of baptism, this Father graciously affirms the choice of his beloved Son. 'As soon as Jesus was baptised he came up from the water, and suddenly the heavens opened and he saw the Spirit of God descending like a dove and coming down on him. And a voice spoke from heaven, "This is my Son, the Beloved; my favour rests on him"' (Mt 3:16-17).

After his baptism, Jesus is led by the Spirit into the wilderness, away once again from the crowds to solitude and prayer. We might have thought that after years of hidden life he would be in a hurry to get into active ministry. His ways are not ours. It is more important to seek his Father from whom he draws all his life and power (Jn 6:57). In the solitude of the desert Jesus will meet his Father, but he will also meet another spirit: Satan, the Tempter, the Accuser, the Prince of Darkness. The name does not matter. The reality cannot be denied.

When goodness and love are chosen as a way of life, another voice soon makes itself heard. It will whisper, distort, accuse, threaten, promise and try to pull us away from the path of love. If Jesus comes to found a kingdom of love in the world, he can expect resistance from the self-styled incumbent. When Jesus chose to identify with sinners in the Jordan, you and I and John did not understand. But Satan understood. By this act of love and compassion Jesus threw down the gauntlet before our ancient enemy. Now Satan picks it up and moves to attack this man who is our champion. Satan fears this man. He fears his hidden way, his humility, his apparent weakness; above all he fears his love. He will now do his utmost to win this man away from this chosen path. He will try to win him over to a strategy we understand better, to miracles, power, achievement and quick results.

'The tempter came and said to him, "If you are the Son of God, tell these stones to turn into loaves"' (Mt 4:3). Jesus has been fasting for many days and is hungry. Another scripture name for Satan is the Accuser. He accuses God of neglecting us and tries to sow doubt in our hearts about God's love. If we are precious to God, how could he allow us to be hungry or to suffer in any way? In a later parable Jesus, speaking of the loving providence of God, asks: 'Is there a man among you who would hand his son a stone when he asked for bread?' (Mt 7:9). Satan here suggests that God has only stones for his hungry son and is neglecting him. But while Jesus is aware of his bodily hunger and need for food just now, he has a deeper need for his Father's love and power. Later he will say that his Father's will is his food. It is this very love relationship between Jesus and his Father that Satan here tries to undermine. We can say he attacks the very identity of Jesus as the beloved Son. He wants Jesus to doubt his Father's love, to doubt if he is who he says he is. 'If you are the Son of God, tell these stones to turn into loaves.'

Up to now Jesus has relied completely on this hidden source of energy, his Father's love. About to enter his public life, he will still depend on this power and not switch over to something more under his own control, a kind of miracle power which will be swift and efficient and make him less dependent on God. This would be to abandon the guiding principle of the plan of salvation, dependence on his Father's love, and to choose to trust in power and miracles instead. This is what Satan wants and fails to get. 'But he replied, "Scripture says, 'Man does not live on bread alone but on every word that comes from the mouth of God'"' (Mt 4:4). The salvation Jesus brings to all of us is something deeper than a mere satisfying of bodily needs. 'Life means more than food' (Lk 12:23). He comes to offer fullness of life, a life flowing from the certainty of God's love for us. What gives our hidden lives of faith their deepest meaning and value is our relationship with God and our trust that he will never abandon us. This trust will be sorely tested at times in our lives. Then the Accuser will say, 'If God loves you, why do these things happen to you?' Jesus understands this. Through the trust he displayed in the desert, he helps us to trust in our time of trial. He does not seek any miracle to escape his hunger. He will work his way through the situation, depending on his Father.

'The devil then took him to the holy city and made him stand on the parapet of the temple. "If you are the Son of God", he said, "throw yourself down; for the scripture says: He will put you in his angels' charge, and they will support you on their hands in case you hurt your foot against a stone"' (Mt 4:5-6). If we are honest, we must admit that this suggestion of Satan excites and attracts us. It seems so plausible. At a moment when the crowd had gathered for worship in the Temple, Jesus could come floating down from above as was expected, and to the Temple as would be appropriate, and stand unhurt among them as the Psalmist had prophesied. Surely it would be a most effective introduction of his mission. There is only thing wrong with it. It is not God's way. He has chosen another way, hidden, slow and humble. This temptation is a direct attack on God's chosen strategy. Jesus will not try to dazzle us with miracles. He invites us to interior conversion of heart and seeks to motivate us to this by love, a love shown by walking the road of trust in his Father. We do not find this an easy path. We prefer miracle, instant bread, glory and acclaim. We want the easy way, the short cut. Jesus has deeper wisdom. He knows that the short cut suggested by Satan leads nowhere. We cannot jump over the difficult patches of life. Jesus will walk our road, trusting only in his Father. Hopefully we will find it easier to walk the same road, knowing that he is with us.

'Next, taking him to a very high mountain, the devil showed him all the kingdoms of the world and their splendour. "I will give you all these," he said, "if you fall at my feet and worship me"' (Mt 4:8-9). This third temptation is less subtle. It's a last desperate assault by Satan who senses that he has met his match in this extraordinary man. He conjures up some kind of global vision in the mind of Jesus. Then, boasting that he has control over all kingdoms, he promises them to Jesus if he will adore him. Again, there is the temptation to take a quick and easy way. Satan here speaks with a cynical worldly wisdom. He is saying to Jesus, 'Save yourself all the trouble. People are not worth it. They don't want your kind of salvation anyway. Don't offer them such a difficult choice. I can give them to you if you join me.' Here is the old temptation to use quick but evil means for a good cause. How much suffering has come about all through history when people give in to this temptation! Jesus stands firm. He will not compromise with evil. He will not drink from a poisoned well, even were he dying of thirst. There is only one spring where he will draw water, only one source of life for him, the love of his Father. 'Then Jesus replied, "Be off, Satan! For Scripture says: you must worship the Lord your God, and serve him alone' (Mt 4:10).

'Then the devil left him, and angels appeared and looked after him' (Mt 4:11). Jesus is now at peace. He stands by the choice he made to live the hidden life in Nazareth and the choice to join us for baptism in the Jordan. He reaffirms these choices by this stand in the desert and thereby sets out on a road that will inevitably lead to Calvary. There he will be lifted up not by guardian angels anxious to save him from hurt, but by men busy crucifying him, still tempting him to doubt his Father's love. On that hill, Satan's deceits will be unmasked and God's wisdom revealed, and his own word will start to bear fruit: 'And when I am lifted up from the earth, I shall draw all people to myself' (Jn 12:32).

10

'REPENT' – INVITATION NOT THREAT

After this desert experience, Jesus begins what we call his 'public life'. This expression is used in contrast to the hidden life of Nazareth. He will now be seen by crowds who will listen to his teaching. He will challenge public figures in authority. He will heal the sick and get the name of wonder-worker. His preaching and lifestyle will give rise to questions and suspicion, and will gradually provoke the opposition and even the hatred of the religious leaders. We must be careful how we interpret this new stage of his life. Jesus does not, as it were, go public like a political activist seeking to attract crowds, to win fans and public support. He is not changing strategy and now opting to rely on publicity and miracles to make up for lost time. For Jesus, his real, true, meaningful life is the life of the heart, the hidden life of personal love for his Father. This is the source of all his power to touch people's hearts and heal their wounds and hurts. He knows the human heart and its real needs. He comes to save us from our sins. This salvation will not be achieved through speeches and miracles but only through love, by helping people to understand that in all their hiddenness and brokenness their lives are rich in meaning because they themselves are loved unconditionally by God.

The evangelists introduce the public ministry of Jesus with a very subdued report. They do not describe any great opening rally or inaugural address. They tell us simply that 'after John had been arrested, Jesus went into Galilee. There he proclaimed the Good News from God. "The time has come," he said, "and the kingdom of God is close at hand, Repent, and believe the Good News"' (Mk 1:14-15). What a contrast with our modern techniques of publicity, propaganda and persuasion. Many political leaders have seen themselves as Messiahs of their people, especially if they have been swept into power by enthusiastic supporters, hungry for change and hoping for the improvement of their hard lives. Such leaders deliver a carefully-prepared speech on inauguration day. They outline a blueprint for a better society. Many promises are made. Some strike a realistic note and call for sacrifice, and the crowd promises to be patient in waiting for better days. But as time passes, new problems

46

and unexpected difficulties appear. The real enemies in the heart – greed, pride, selfishness and corruption – have not been overcome. These hidden forces frustrate our plans and smash our dreams.

We are reflecting on the first Messiah. His people, the Jews, had lived in expectation of his coming and his saving power. Their history was full of oppression and suffering. Their Messiah would subdue their enemies and restore their fortunes. So they dreamed. But God also had dreams, not just for one race but for all people, for you and me. And as always, his dreams are as high above ours as the heavens are above the earth. He has come to identify and destroy the real enemies of all people. He has come to show us the way to true and lasting peace, joy and happiness. He will unmask those hidden enemies – fear, greed, selfishness and pride – and give us power to overcome them. He will not do this by any kind of coercion, by imposing laws and sanctions, but by unveiling a great beauty hiding among us, a powerful hidden force lying in our very hearts, the beauty and the power of God's everlasting and unfailing love.

It is this love which is at the heart and centre of all his preaching. Jesus does not threaten, scold or warn of the consequences of refusing to adore God. He does not stress commandments or the punishment that could fall on those who break them. He speaks of the 'kingdom of God', which for him meant the active presence of God among us. This God works on our behalf, caring, healing, renewing and liberating. Jesus called this message 'Good News'. 'News' suggests something dynamic, something happening, something going on around us which we did not start or initiate. That news is the presence of this working God among us, a God who has not rejected us because of our sins and failures, a God who comes close in compassion, as close as Jesus had come to those people in the Jordan. In one sermon, after describing the kind of thing God is doing, bringing liberty to captives, sight to the blind, freedom to the downtrodden, Jesus says to his listeners, 'This text is being fulfilled today even as you listen' (Lk 4:22).

Jesus speaks more about what God wants to do or is doing for us than about what we have to do to please him. We may ask if we have nothing to do. Surely God's activity will not be imposed on us? Yes, we have something to do and, if we don't do it, the kingdom cannot touch us and we will not experience the Good News. Jesus tells us in that short opening word of his preaching what we must do. 'The kingdom of God is close at hand. Repent, and believe the Good News' (Mk 1:15). We have to repent. Let us look at this word 'repent'. It is a very rich word but is often misunderstood. It comes across to most people as a negative word, frightening, more like a threat and certainly not like good news.

What thoughts come into your mind when you hear this word? I used to think that it meant 'give up that sin', or 'do penance for your sins', or 'break that bad habit'. The further suggestion in my mind was that I had to carry out this daunting programme by my own efforts! And when I had fulfilled those difficult conditions God would love me. For me that was not good news. That was what I had always thought anyway, that I must by my own efforts give up sin as a condition for receiving God's love. Is Jesus only repeating what I had always believed about my sinful self and the holy God and our relationship? No, Jesus is not repeating our poor idea of God and his love and goodness. Our old idea was bad news. Jesus comes with the inside story, the good news, the truth that can set us free (Jn 8:32).

The truth, the good news, is that God loves me as I am now, as I read these lines, and comes close to me now before I change. This closeness and love, given before I change, release the power to overcome sin. To experience that power Jesus says I must 'repent'. This simply means that I must turn around and look at him. The literal meaning of this word 'repent' is 'to turn around, to look in a new direction'. Jesus asks us to turn around, to look into his eyes and to believe that he loves us. He asks me to look at him and to let him look at me, maybe as he looked at Peter after Peter's denials. This look may reduce me to tears, but they will be tears of love, even joy, which will heal and renew me. Jesus asks me to stop looking at my sin and failure, to stop looking into the eyes of Pharisees and other judges. In his eyes alone will I find the truth which will bring healing and liberation.

The word 'repent' is not a threat but a beautiful invitation. When I accept the invitation and look at him, I will see that there is no condemnation, no judgement, but only understanding, compassion, forgiveness and desire for friendship. This will release all the energy I need to cope with sin and failure. 'The saint is a sinner who knows he or she is forgiven.' Jesus came with this good news because our human ideas about repenting were false. We cannot by our own efforts alone give up sin, reform, break bad habits and grow in love. That's why Jesus came. In preaching this good news to the people he is simply sharing with them his own inner life, that which gave all the meaning and power to his own life, his love relationship with his Father. He wants to lead us all into awareness of that same love in our own lives. He wants to help us to discover the treasure buried in the field of our lives, buried under layers of dull routine, personal sin and failure, fear and doubt. This is the good news. Indeed Jesus himself is the Good News. He is the guarantee of the message he brings. He will die rather than abandon this mission or change this message.

11

ANYBODY AT HOME?

In a sermon in the synagogue in Nazareth, Jesus chose a text from Isaiah which foretold all that God would do for his people through the Messiah. When Isaiah spoke the words they were prophecy. When Jesus spoke them in Nazareth they had become facts, news, the kingdom of God among us. After he read the text of Isaiah and prepared to speak all eyes in the synagogue were fixed on him. 'Then he began to speak to them, "This text is being fulfilled today even as you listen"' (Lk 4:22). Let us, his followers of today, now ask ourselves a simple but pertinent question: 'Do I listen?' Do I really listen to the good news? Will I repent, turn around and look into the eyes of Jesus? Will I receive this Messiah who comes to my heart with the good news? He seeks my friendship, my love. Will I spend some time with him in prayer? How will I get to know him, if I don't spend some time with him? How will I hear his message of good news if I don't open the door of my heart, invite him in and sit at his feet as Mary did at Bethany? This is prayer. I do not speak here of saying vocal prayers but of that quiet prayer of the heart we call contemplation.

In his farewell discourse at the Last Supper, Jesus describes the intimacy God offers us in prayer with these words:

> If anyone loves me he will keep my word, and my
> Father will love him, and we shall come to him and
> make our home with him.
>
> Jn 14:23

How gracious that Jesus should choose this image and speak of our hearts as his home. In Nazareth he experienced home life for many years. He is personally aware of all the beautiful human experiences we associate with this rich image. Home is that place where we feel secure, where we feel accepted and loved, a place of joyful memories. There we are in touch with our roots. Our sense of personal identity is strengthened by the knowledge that we belong to a family. We are relaxed and at ease at home. But as I write these words I am very conscious that this is not everybody's experience and that many have no such joyful memories of home.

For many home has been a place of tension, a place where they have experienced rejection rather than loving acceptance. This is a painful reality which we cannot deny. What can we say? When we hear of the experience of such pain and hurt in that place which should be the most loving, we feel sad and concerned and we try to offer sympathy and love. Now, if we who are weak and sinful feel this way, what about Jesus? Will he not be full of compassion? Will he not want to come in a special way to such people and make his home in their hearts and bring them a deep experience of being loved and accepted. To such people especially Jesus says that he and his Father consider their hearts as home.

But God will not force his way into anybody's heart. We must invite him in. We must open the door when he knocks. 'Look, I am standing at the door, knocking. If one of you hears me calling and opens the door, I will come in to share his meal, side by side with him' (Rv 3:20). Perhaps we feel unworthy of his visit. Let us remember that he knows us as we are and comes to us as we are. This is the good news.

One morning, while praying on those words from Revelation, 'Look I am standing at the door, knocking,' the following dialogue arose in my heart:

Jesus: Behold, I stand at the door and knock.
Me: Who are you?

Jesus: I am Jesus.
Me: What do you want?

Jesus: I have a message for you.
Me: What is your message?

Jesus: It's hard to tell with all the noise out here.
Will you let me in?
Me: I fear your message.

Jesus: Do not fear. I have good news for you.
Me: Good news? Have I won something?

Jesus: Yes. You have won God's favour and love.
Me: That cannot be true!

Jesus: I who speak to you am the Truth.
Me: You've come to the wrong house.

Jesus: No, I'm sure of the address. I got it from my Father's heart.
Me: I can't believe that.

Jesus: If you let me in I will prove it.
Me: How will you prove it?

Jesus: I will show you the wounds in my hands.
Me: But you will blame me and my sins for those wounds.

Jesus: No. I will tell you I would gladly go through all that again if it would convince you of my love. Will you let me in?
Me: I'm afraid and I'm ashamed.

Jesus: Why?
Me: It's very dirty in here. It's no place for someone like you.

Jesus: But it's in there in your heart that I most want to be.
Me: But you have no idea of how dark and dirty it is in here.

Jesus: I have every idea. I know every bit of dirt and sin in your house.
Me: Then why on earth do you want to come in?

Jesus: Because I love you.

We find it hard to believe that God really desires our company and almost impossible to believe that he rejoices to be with us in prayer. But that is the good news. We are so hung up on the idea of our unworthiness, even though the whole of Revelation in scripture tells us that God first loved us. In *Letters from the Desert* Carlo Carretto tells us why he keeps praying. 'It is not I who wanted prayer. It is he who wanted it. It is not I who have looked for him. It is he who has looked for me first. My seeking him would have been in vain if, before all time, he had not sought me.' Before all time God has sought me, not because I am worthy, but because I am his and precious in his sight and he loves me (Is 43). It's really so simple! Earlier I said that a quiet secluded spot or the company of a loving friend can be true images of prayer. Jesus himself is that place of rest and he is that friend. 'I call you friends, because I have made known to you everything I have learnt from my Father' (Jn 15:15). He invites us to 'make your home in me, as I make mine in you' (Jn 15:4). No journey is necessary to reach this place of rest or to meet this friend.

In Deuteronomy Moses reminds the chosen people of their great privilege and good fortune in having the word of God's guiding law imprinted on their hearts. He points out that there is no need for anyone to go up to heaven to bring down the word. Nor need they ask anyone to cross the sea to bring it back. Such journeys are not necessary because 'the word is very near to you, it is in your heart for your observance' (Dt 30:14). Moses is speaking here of the word of God's law. He never could have imagined the immense good fortune of God's people in a later time when God would speak a new word, his clearest word of love, Jesus. And this word of love become flesh, this Jesus, would delight to live in our inmost hearts and call them his home.

In the gospel we read the story of the Roman centurion who asked Jesus to heal his servant. Jesus set out for the man's house. When this pagan soldier heard that Jesus was actually on the way to his house, he sent messengers saying that he was unworthy that Jesus should enter his home and that it would be enough if Jesus just said the word and his servant would be healed (Lk 7:7). Maybe God read our hearts which feel so unworthy to have him in our homes. It is as if we said to God: 'You don't have to come to our house, to our world, to heal our brokenness. You are God. Just say the word and our world will be healed.' But God really wanted to come, not just to visit but to stay. And so he got around the problem by saying a very special and unexpected word. It was a word of such intense caring and compassion that it became flesh in Jesus. Because of this miracle of love God is with us always in Jesus, even to the end of time.

But despite God's great desire to make his home in our hearts, he will not force himself on us. 'Look, I am standing at the doo,r knocking.' If we open the door and invite him in, he will sit with us. He will listen to us and hopes that we will listen to him. He knows us better than we know ourselves. We won't have to do much explaining. Often it will be enough to ask him just to look at us. His look alone can heal us. He will be relaxed with us and help

53

us feel relaxed with him. Give him time. He has treasure to share with us. That treasure is the inner hidden meaning of our lives. Treasure is not found lying on the surface of a field. It is usually buried, hidden. We have to do some digging. We must make an effort. If we believe that there is treasure there, we will make sacrifices. If we become serious about prayer, we will find it involves some sacrifice, but when we find the treasure, the sacrifice will be as nothing.

12

PARABLES – MORE THAN STORIES

Jesus calls us friends. When friends are together they talk about the deeper things, those things that give meaning to life. They share secrets, those hidden experiences and feelings which are the source of their joys and sorrows. The greatest force in Jesus's life is his love for his Father. So we are not surprised that he wants to tell us about that love, his big secret. 'No one knows who the Father is except the Son and those to whom the Son chooses to reveal him' (Lk 10:22). In prayer the Son wants to reveal the Father to us. 'I call you friends, because I have made known to you everything I have learnt from my Father' (Jn 15:15).

When Jesus seeks to reveal the Father to us, he faces some problems. One of these is that we may think that we already know what God is like and so we won't really listen. We have our own fixed ideas about God, how he thinks, feels and acts. This can make us deaf to the truth which can only come from Jesus. The theologian Paul Tillich speaks in one of his sermons of waiting on God, waiting for God to reveal himself. He says we all find this difficult because we think that we know and possess God. He lists different people who may think this way: the theologian thinks she knows God through doctrines; the Bible student thinks he knows God through the Bible; the churchman thinks that he knows God through the institutional Church; and the believer thinks she knows God through her spiritual experience. But God cannot be known or possessed like that. God is infinite mystery. Do we not find it hard to know another person, even to know ourselves? What then about God? We must enter prayer with a very humble, open attitude, ready to let Jesus teach us, surprise us, delight us and humble us. Our exploration of the Mystery of God will go on for the whole of our lifetime of prayer.

Another problem Jesus faces in trying to tell us about God is that of language. How can our weak human words describe in any adequate way the mystery of God, the wonder of his being, his beauty, his love? All the great saints and mystics who try to tell us of their experience of God in prayer confess their utter sense of hopelessness. They end up saying such things as, 'What we say about God is more untrue than true'; or 'Those who know, don't say; those who say, don't know'; or 'If you describe him, then what you describe is not God.' These holy people are not saying that we cannot know God or talk about him. They just remind us that God is infinitely more wonderful than our poor words can suggest. They warn us that we must never think that we can 'measure' God. As a true human person Jesus has to accept the limitations of our speech. But the good news is that he has come to reveal God his Father to us. He is motivated by love, his deep love for his Father and for us. Also, as he speaks to our hearts, he gives us his Holy Spirit to enlighten us, to make his words live and act in us, so that we can enter prayer with great confidence.

Let us notice some of the ways Jesus uses human language which represent an effort to cope with this problem of speaking about the mystery of God in weak human words. We will consider here his use of parables and exaggeration and, later, his use of paradox. Jesus frequently used parables in teaching about the mysteries of the kingdom of God. In using parables he is not just adapting himself to a mostly illiterate audience of simple rural folk used to story-telling. There is much more to it than that. Indeed, at one point, people complained about his excessive use of parables and asked why he would not speak more openly. Many teachers use the story as a teaching method and it was common in Jesus' day. But the parables of Jesus are more than a good teaching instrument. They are a treasure house of divine revelation. They are the fruit of his own communication with his Father through long hidden years in Nazareth. 'My teaching is not from myself; it comes from the one who sent me' (Jn 7:16). In prayer today we can listen to that teaching and explore the treasure house.

In Scripture the word of God is described as an active, lifegiving agent (Is 55:11). In the parables Jesus is not simply giving us information about God. The parables are not like stories offered as illustrations of catechism lessons. Jesus does not just offer knowledge for the mind but communicates the very life of God for our whole person. 'I have come so that they may have life and have it to the full' (Jn 10:10). In exploring the parables we seek not so much to understand some teaching but rather to be put in touch with God's life. We are dealing more with heart-knowledge than head-knowledge. The stories are more about living than learning, about loving than understanding. We do not seek to understand God as someone 'out there', independent of us and of

what is going on right now in our lives. The parables deal with the
mystery of God but also with the mystery of ourselves and of our
relationship with him.

Therefore, if we are to be nourished by these lifegiving stories,
we must find ourselves in them. We will lose their power if we
remain outside them. A great variety of characters appear in the
parables but God and myself are the chief actors. The parable will
not touch me, heal me, reveal God to me if I stand outside it and
judge those who appear in the story. We begin by hearing a story
about others but then we must move into the story.

In the Book of Samuel we read how David sinned seriously by
taking another man's wife and having her husband killed. God sent
the prophet Nathan to David to call him to repentance. Nathan told
David a parable about a rich man who had many flocks and herds.
A traveller visited the rich man who, instead of feeding him with an
animal from his own herds, went and stole the only lamb of a poor
neighbouring farmer. David listened to the story. Then we are told,
'David's anger flared up against the man. "As Yahweh lives," he
said, "the man who did this deserves to die!" Then Nathan said to
David, "You are the man"' (II S 12:5-7).

We are not meant to judge the people in the parable; rather the
parable judges us. We have to identify ourselves in these stories. And
We will do this differently according to our different situations. As
the years pass by and we gain more experience of life, we will,
under the guidance of the Spirit, find new meaning and
nourishment in these life-giving stories.

There is a feature common to many parables, that of
exaggeration. We have said that in revealing his Father to us, Jesus
faced the problem that we all have preconceived ideas about God.
We think that we know what he is like. We transfer our ideas to
God and end up with a small God. Thus we can cut ourselves off
from the amazing power he offers us. In his stories Jesus
deliberately exaggerates to shake us out of this complacency and
help us to see that we do not and cannot realise how good God is.
Consider some examples of this feature of his story-telling. The
greatest parable about the mercy of God is the story of the prodigal
son. The title 'prodigal son' is a terrible misnomer. The central
character in this story is not the son but the father. Jesus tells the
story precisely to reveal his Father. A much better title would be
the 'prodigal father', because in the story it is the father who is
prodigal, wasteful of affection, mercy and love. All through the

story Jesus makes the father act in a highly exaggerated way. He gives his younger son the inheritance without any question. When the boy has gone, the father watches every day for his return. On the day he returns, the father runs down the road to welcome him. He embraces the boy in his rags, does not listen to his confession, orders the best robe to be brought out on to the road and has the best animal on the farm killed for a celebration (Lk 15:11-32).

This kind of exaggeration occurs in many stories. In the parable of the lost sheep, the shepherd leaves ninety-nine good sheep unprotected while he heads off into the desert to search for one foolish stray (Lk 15:4-7). In the story of the unforgiving debtor, Jesus describes a servant who, having just been forgiven an immense debt by his master, immediately pounces on a fellow servant, beats him and has him thrown into prison for failing to pay a tiny debt (Mt 18:23-25). Another story describes an employer hiring people to work in his vineyard at different hours of the day. Some start at the beginning of the day, others are hired at the end of the day, but all receive the same pay! (Mt 20:1-16). In another vineyard story, the workers not only refuse to hand over the produce to the owner but even kill his son who comes to collect it (Mt 21:33-43). We all love the story of the Good Samaritan but must wonder how the beaten traveller is spurned by fellow Jews and clerics to boot and is then helped in a quite exaggerated way by a Samaritan, a foreigner and traditional enemy of the Jew. (Lk 10:29-37).

I believe that to become aware of the exaggeration and even to become annoyed with it is the beginning of learning, the beginning of entry into discovery of the wonder of God and his ways. I believe Jesus expects us to be annoyed with that father in the story of the prodigal son and with the way he treats the two sons. He expects us to feel sorry for the elder son in that story and for those early workers in the vineyard. He expects us to be angry with that unforgiving servant who threw his workmate into prison. In general, Jesus expects us to react as David did to Nathan's story! That's why the stories are told: to lead us to search our own hearts. The trouble is that we often stop at the point of judging those in the parable. We all need a Nathan to whisper in our ears, 'You are that man.' In prayer, if we are searching for God, I believe that the Holy Spirit will be our Nathan. Jesus promised us the Spirit as a helper in prayer (Jn 14:26). The Spirit will help us to understand what Jesus taught.

Our reaction of annoyance and even judgment to many parables is our way of saying that 'this does not apply to me'. When we judge the father for being too soft with the prodigal son, we cannot imagine that we ourselves might ever be in need of such mercy – we would not go that far! When we judge him for being unfair to the elder son, we cannot believe that in fact the whole farm belongs to that elder boy, that all of heaven and earth are given to me as gift by a God who loves me as his child. When I complain about the father or the vineyard owner over their exaggerated generosity to failures and lazy people, I am saying, 'I would not act like that, encouraging sin and irresponsibility.' Jesus is smiling and saying, 'I know that. That's what I have to tell you, that God's ways are above yours.' When I am angry with the unforgiving servant, I am saying, 'I would never behave like that.' But Jesus is saying, 'That man is you!' It's just that you and I have never really believed that we have been totally forgiven everything by God. And when I think the Good Samaritan overdid it, maybe it's because I know, as I am asked by Jesus at the end of the story, that I should 'Go, and do the same yourself' (Lk 10:37).

Jesus came to reveal the mystery of God and love. To enter the mystery and be nourished by it, we need time and prayer. Mystery does not mean absence of meaning or unattainable meaning, but meaning so rich that time is needed to explore it. The parables of Jesus are for all time. His teaching is an eternal word spoken to us today. Jesus seeks to draw us into these stories and in that way to draw us into the life-giving stream of his healing love where the hidden life we share with him can be nourished.

13

MIRACLES OR MIRACLE?

To every single person Jesus says, 'I have come that you may have life and have it to the full' (Jn 10:10). That fullness of life is not to be measured by any spectacular externals. It is a hidden treasure. It is not some new wonder imported by Jesus from heaven. It is something already within us which he now reveals to us. He opens our eyes to where our true value, beauty and meaning lie. They lie within us and not in wealth, fame and achievement. Jesus conveys to people God's loving acceptance of them as they are. He touches the lives of ordinary, humble, even sinful folk at deep levels. Many are transformed. The marginalised and outcasts and sinners find treasure within themselves, hidden under their apparent nothingness, failure and rejection by society. People oppressed by strange dark forces are delivered and find their true selves. Jesus speaks the truth and points to hidden beauty, and since the human spirit is made for truth and beauty, it responds. Many people touched in that way experience a freedom from and a healing of a variety of ills of body and spirit. Miracles happen.

How do we see these miracles? Do they contradict what we have been saying about the hidden life of Jesus? Are they a new strategy to persuade and convince and win converts? Do we think that Jesus in working miracles is in some way giving in to the temptation in the desert, 'change these stones to bread', or 'cast yourself down'? Is he now looking for the quick, easy way to make up for lost time? To ask such questions is really to answer them, but it is good to ask the questions, since they invite us to look at the deeper meaning of the miracles in the life of Jesus. I used to think that Jesus worked miracles to convince people that he was more than man, to prove his identity as Messiah. I now see how childish this idea was and how it missed completely the true wonder of Jesus, the real meaning of his life and, indeed, the true meaning and wonder of my own life.

Jesus did not set out to convert people by displays of power, by miracles in that sense. He sought a conversion deeper than any mere surface sense of wonder. He sought to convert our hearts by love and invited a free response of love. He would not try to manipulate us by wonders and spectacles. Indeed we can say that

Jesus put no trust in signs and wonders. He knows the human heart too well. Many times in the gospels, when he healed someone, he would warn the person not to publicise the healing. Why? Because he knows how easily people will follow a wonder-worker for very wrong and selfish motives. He has come precisely to deliver us from selfishness. Jesus seeks a deeper conversion, not a shallow conversion based on emotions, excitement, even selfishness. This would wear off when trouble, sickness or misfortune came and there was no miracle to rescue us.

When Jesus feeds the crowd in the desert, he is very upset by the excited popular reaction of the crowd to the miracle. They want to make him king. 'Jesus, who could see they were about to come and take him by force and make him king, escaped back to the hills by himself' (Jn 6:15). What a curious bit of drama! I imagine Jesus sensing the mood, then slipping away through the bushes and rocks and looking back over his shoulder. He finds a small cave and hides till he hears the crowd moving off. John uses the word 'escaped'. Jesus, he says, had to escape from the crowd. Usually when you read of someone escaping from a pursuing crowd, you think of a person in danger of being beaten, even killed. But this crowd wants to make Jesus their king! The word 'escape' here tells us much about Jesus and his mission among us. He has not come for the power and glory which this crowd would associate with kingship. He has come not to be served but to serve. Love is at the heart of his mission. This crowd would not understand that their enthusiasm to make him a popular king was a more serious danger to his mission than if they were chasing him with sticks and stones in their hands. Jesus has to escape from a popularity which any modern public leader would relish. It was a serious threat to his mission, which was to give fullness of life to his people. And life is more than bread.

Jesus fed the crowd out of human compassion for their hunger, not to win popular support. He will not let the people impose on him their kind of kingship. Like us, these people also had their preconceived ideas of God and had cast a role for their Messiah, a king of power who would crush their enemies and make them great. But God has more wonderful dreams for them and for us. Yes, Jesus is a king. The angel spoke about this before his birth and prophets foretold it, but he will be God's kind of king, a king of love. This title he will earn not by the spectacular miracle of multiplying food but by nourishing our deepest hunger, our need to be loved as we are. This leads to the deep conversion. When we believe this incredibly good news then, hopefully, we can be converted. Notice that the word 'conversion', like the word 'repent', also means to turn around, to face in a new direction, to look into the eyes of God and see his love for us and accept it.

The miracles are displays not of power but of love. Maybe we should say they are displays of the power of love. When Jesus heals the leper, he is not trying to show his power over disease and thus prove that he is God. This would be 'using' the sick man, the very contradiction of love. Genuine love could not use someone in this way. He cured the leper because he loved the man (Mt 8:1-4). He places his hands on the woman bent double for eighteen years because he is moved by compassion and says it is not right that she should remain thus bound by Satan (Lk 13:10-17). What Jesus reveals in the miracles is the love of God which is, of course, the real power of God. The miracle is an evangelical event, evidence of the good news that God cares for and loves us and is moved by our sufferings. But if the human heart is not in some way in tune with what Jesus stands for, then the miracle loses its power to evangelise. When Caiaphas heard the news of the raising of Lazarus from the dead, not only was he not converted, but he even plotted to have Lazarus killed to remove the evidence of the miracle (Jn 12:10-11). Again, when Jesus delivered some unfortunate people from evil spirits, his enemies were not impressed but said simply that this was proof that Jesus was in league with Satan.

This reflection helps me to understand something that used to puzzle me. Why did Jesus not appear to his enemies and accusers after he rose from the dead? Surely Caiaphas and Pilate would have been converted if Jesus had appeared to them after he rose. This idea was very attractive to me and again revealed how little I understood God's ways. To me it seemed like good drama guaranteed to bring good results. I see now that Jesus could never try to convert in this way, because he seeks love. He will not impose himself on us by wonders and thus force us to accept him. Also, Jesus knows the human heart too well. He knew that such an appearance would not affect Caiaphas or Pilate. In one of his parables Jesus uses these words: 'If they will not listen either to Moses or to the prophets, they will not be convinced even if someone should rise from the dead' (Lk 16:31). Had Jesus appeared to Caiaphas or Pilate, they would simply have sought to kill him again and make even more sure this time. Only eyes of faith and love can 'see' the risen Lord.

Jesus did not use miracles either to make his own personal life easier or to impress people and get results in his public ministry. In fact he did not 'use' miracles at all. He was moved to compassion by human suffering and then, by his tremendous empathy, he evoked great faith in sufferers which seemed to touch and release a healing energy which cured many. People did not understand this and so, when he hung on the cross, he was mocked for not using miraculous power to save himself. The chief priests and the scribes mocked him among themselves in the same way. "He saved others," they said, "he cannot save himself" (Mk 15:31). What they failed to realise was that it was the very same force of love that was at work in both of these situations. It was his great love that saved many people in a variety of healing miracles. It was this very same love that restrained any miraculous delivery of himself from the cross. As some saints say, it was this very love that kept him on the cross, not nails or ropes. His endurance of the pain and shame of death on a cross was the greatest proof of his love. This was the greatest miracle of all. There could be no greater wonder than this love and it had the power to save the whole world.

On one occasion, three of his disciples were privileged to be with Jesus on the mountainside when he was transfigured before them in prayer. Overawed, they bowed their faces to the ground. When the moment of glory passed, they raised their heads and, we are told, 'they saw no one there but Jesus' (Mt 17:8). All through his public life and ministry, Jesus resists publicity and glory. He is known as the carpenter. People see 'no one but Jesus'. He reveals daily love and caring and not any blinding light or glory. Why did he take these three disciples with him on that occasion of the transfiguration? Perhaps to encourage them and strengthen them for the coming passion. But in case they began to get any wrong impression, Jesus spoke to them on the way down from the mountain, warning them to tell no one what they had seen. Then he spoke of his forthcoming suffering and death. This is the other sure road into the hearts of people, not a road of miracles or glory, but a road of love proved by suffering and death. This is a hidden way but a sure one.

14

JESUS – THE PARADOX OF GOD

Jesus sought to win our hearts not with miracles but with love. The greatest revelation of that love was Calvary. This was his most powerful miracle. I wish to reflect on Calvary and to introduce the reflection with a word on 'paradox'. The dictionary defines paradox as 'a statement which appears absurd and self-contradictory but which has a hidden truth'. Jesus frequently spoke in paradox: 'For the least among you all, that is the one who is great.' 'Anyone who finds his life will lose it.' 'If anyone believes in me, even though he dies he will live.' 'If anyone wants to be first, he must make himself last of all.' Many people find these and other similar sayings difficult, even annoying, and are tempted to neglect them. But while paradox may not be part of normal daily speech and even offends our sense of logic, we still sense that, deep down, rich truth is hiding there. We are made for truth and something deep within us echoes that hidden truth.

I think that the dictionary definition of paradox does not do justice to its real significance. We use language daily to communicate ordinary ideas and feelings. But we use language more seriously when speaking of deeper, more complex matters. Language is meant to reflect reality, the mystery of life, but reality is too rich and complex to be captured in neat definition. I mentioned the problem of saints trying to talk about their experience of God and the problem Jesus had in trying to tell us of his Father's love, namely that our words are too weak to describe the mystery. We noted how Jesus used parable and exaggeration to help communicate the mystery of God. His use of paradox is another attempt to overcome the limitations of language. Paradox combines opposites and offends our logic, which says that if something is small, this excludes the possibility that it is great, or that if it is described as first, it cannot be last. But the reality which language describes is itself very complex and full of ambiguity, and so paradox will often come closer to revealing truth than more straightforward language. Consider a lighter example from G.K. Chesterton, a master of paradox. Asked on one occasion if he believed in ghosts, he said, 'Certainly not, but I am quite scared of them!' Most of us can identify with what he says here. Not wishing to be described as superstitious, we would protest that we do not believe in ghosts, but if we were passing a graveyard at night on a lonely road, we would probably quicken our step! Chesterton's paradox neatly communicates this complexity and ambiguity of the human person.

Jesus does not use paradox merely to emphasise a point, just as he does not use parables merely as a teaching method. When he tells a parable, he asks people not just to listen to a story but to enter into a personal experience of the mystery. Thus, with paradox, when he says that if you want to be first you must be last, he invites us to live out the word. Only then will we be able to experience the truth hiding there. This was his own experience. In fact it is only when we contemplate his experience, especially the central experience of his passion and death, that we can begin to appreciate the truth hiding in his parables and paradoxes. Jesus is the word of God made flesh. We can say he is God's final solution to the problem of language. Jesus himself is the Good News. He is God's greatest parable, his most startling paradox. Here is a parable not in words, but in deeds of self-sacrificing love to the point of death. 'A man can have no greater love than to lay down his life for his friends' (Jn 15:13). We can say that a man can find no greater language than this to tell someone 'I love you.' Jesus is the great paradox of God made flesh. He who is first in his Father's heart is last in human estimation on Calvary. He who in heaven's eye is greatest is now the least among us. He who is our Lord and master is now servant of us all. He who is author of life now hides in death and this death brings life to the world forever.

Here is his highest achievement, the completion of the plan of salvation hidden from all eternity. Now Satan, sin, fear and guilt are all overcome by this total self-emptying love of Jesus and he can say from the cross, 'It is accomplished' (Jn 19:30). Again, another paradox. His task is 'achieved' by his suffering and death, a great passive act, an act of surrender, of allowing others to do to him as they will. He does not overthrow or confound his enemies with force or power. But this death on the cross, the most passive act imaginable, is the most powerful agent of change in all history. Once again the deepest reality is hidden. It all happens in a public place, on a hill by the roadside, but the glory is hidden. Yet this is the glory. The glory is not something consequent on the suffering and death, not like a reward for his bravery. The glory is in the sacrifice; not so much in the pain and humiliation but in the total surrender to the Father whom Jesus knows is Love.

All was not as it seemed that Friday on Calvary. More was happening than met the eye. We have been noticing how deeper reality is very much a hidden thing, not found on life's surface. The hidden life of Jesus did not end when he left Nazareth. He is always a hiding God. Here again, on Calvary, the great reality is hidden. Up to this the Jews had a problem because their Messiah turned out to be a carpenter. Now, on this hill, the carpenter is back to his familiar wood, hammer and nails, but he does not have control even over these humble tools. In fact they are turned against him by men. Now the poor Jews have to discover their Messiah under this new and terrible disguise. 'Cursed be everyone who is hanged on a tree' (Ga 3:13). Not many people 'saw' the deeper reality that day. Certainly not the people you would have expected, not the 'religious' people. It was the unlikely ones who were in touch with reality. The gospels mention two such people, a pagan Roman officer and a Jewish criminal executed beside Jesus.

These two rough and simple men speak words of great depth. While the chief priests and elders mock Jesus' claim to be the Son of God with cruel words, 'Let God rescue him if he wants him. For he did say: "I am the Son of God"' (Mt 27:44), the pagan soldier confesses, 'In truth this man was a son of God' (Mk 15:39). And while the religious leaders are furious at the title 'King of the Jews' which Pilate had nailed in mockery on the cross, the Jewish criminal dying beside Jesus made the great act of faith that in fact Jesus was a king, and asked to be remembered when Jesus entered his kingdom. What had these men seen that had opened their eyes? St Mark says it was the way Jesus had died. Both men marvel that this innocent man dies in such a totally forgiving, loving way. How fitting that on that day the two voices raised in defence of Jesus were those of men whom the self-righteous would class as 'sinners', but whom Jesus would be glad to call friends. On that hill have not the last become first?

When St Paul speaks of the mystery of Calvary, he too uses paradox and writes, 'God's foolishness is wiser than human wisdom and God's weakness is stronger than human strength' (I Co 1:25). These words remind us again that appearances are often deceptive. Anyone passing Calvary that afternoon would see only foolishness and weakness. Paul looks deeper and says that hiding there for all who will search is the wisdom and power of God. In what way can this be wisdom and power? Our human wisdom says suffering and death are evil. Suffering must be avoided at all costs and death must be postponed as long as possible. Our wisdom also says that God, by definition, cannot suffer. If he could suffer or die he would cease to be God. But Jesus is the wisdom of God and here he says to us that suffering and death, when they come freely out of love, can generate life and beauty. Such love does not and cannot die. Jesus says all things are possible to God, even to suffer and die! Because we whom he loves suffer and die, so he wants to be with us in this. This is his wisdom. And because in this way he is saying, 'I love you so much, I want to die for you', a new power that can cope with anything in life is released in us, the power of love.

Jesus is the truth. Since we are made for truth, something deep within us echoes to his word, agrees with it and says it must be so. If God is really God, he must share our suffering and death. Somehow, if he did not enter our suffering, even our death, we would have to say he cannot be God. If God is love and love shares all, he must be able to suffer and die with us. Thus all our suffering is in some way saved, redeemed by this loving presence: the cancer and AIDS, the cot death, the fatal accident caused by a drunken driver, the divorce, the public failure; and then the litany of hidden suffering known only to our own hearts: fear, loneliness, pride, rejected love, infidelity, depression. All this is in some wonderful way saved from being wasted or being meaningless because of the presence of our God freely choosing to suffer with us, thus telling our hearts that he knows, he cares, he is near and offers us the power of his love. The French novelist Mauriac says it well: 'I believe as I did as a child that life has meaning, a direction, a value; that no suffering is lost, that every tear counts, each drop of blood; that the secret of the world is to be found in St John's words, "God is Love".'

As the crucifixion of Jesus was a stumbling-block to the faith of the Jews, we can say that the crucifixion of the innocent of our world is a stumbling-block to the faith of many today. The cruel suffering of the poor and innocent caused by the injustices of our world has killed God for many. A well-known personality, interviewed on TV, when asked about her religious belief, answered briefly that 'religion died for me in the mud of Flanders'. Elie Wiesel, describing his thoughts in an extermination camp as

* I have known many men who have said to me that

he watched the smoke rise at night from the chimneys of the crematoria, says, 'Never shall I forget those moments which murdered my God and my soul.' Today, when we look at the images of innocent suffering, too common on our TV screens, those staring, skeleton-faced babies, the bloated bodies, the lines of helpless, hopeless refugees innocent of all crime, I feel that the real hurt in us is not really for the pain of those people. They are too many and we just cannot absorb it all. A deeper pain may be the questioning within us. Can there be a God who is love? Is each baby infinitely precious? Do I not share some responsibility for all this?

Faced with this injustice and the suffering of so many innocents in our world, I believe we must either deny God or totally, humbly and joyfully accept the strange and wonderful wisdom and power revealed on Calvary. Jesus there reveals the inmost being of God, which is love. Because God is compassionate love he freely enters into our pain and suffering and death. That is the wisdom of God and the only meaning of Calvary. If we are convinced of this love, we shall discover power which will enable us to keep going, to keep believing in love as the deepest reality. We will find power to walk the dark road without allowing the darkness to overcome us, power to encounter evil and to respond not with hate but with love as Jesus did. Our love contribution may be small in our eyes, but in his eyes it will be great. United with his enduring love and that of other believers, our love can contribute to the saving and healing of this world. There is no other way.

15

SACRAMENT OF POWERLESSNESS

On Calvary the true interior life of Christ was hidden under the mask of pain, rejection and failure. His true life of love for his Father and for us flowed deep and strong, despite all the storms on the surface. According to Paul, this inner hidden life of Jesus on Calvary is a source of wisdom and power for all who know and follow him. I wish to consider one group of people for whom these reflections have special significance, namely, the sick. Paul's words apply with special force to them: 'The life you have is hidden with Christ in God' (Col 3:3). To the sick I would also dare to apply those words of Jesus: 'I have come so that they may have life and have it to the full' (Jn 10:10). Clearly these words invite us, as does Calvary, to go past externals, to dig deep and search for living water, for true life. Jesus offers 'fullness of life' which is not to be equated with physical well-being, good health, being in control, achieving. This book constantly invites us to reject worldly wisdom which judges by externals and to seek the wisdom of God.

'I have come so that they may have life and have it to the full.' In what imaginable way can these words apply to the sick? The first thing we can say is that the suffering of Jesus on Calvary in some way redeems the apparent meaninglessness of our sickness and suffering. One of the most destructive aspects of human sickness and pain is that it lacks all meaning. It is waste. It can destroy not only the body but the spirit. It is a very dark area with no light. But now a man comes along who is also the Son of God. He says he is the light of the world. He bases his whole life on love and trust. He lives solely out of love for his Father and for us. This kind of living brings him to Calvary, and he who is light and love enters that dark place, enduring with courage, love and trust, and his spirit is not overcome by the dark.

This Jesus once said that no one lights a lamp and then hides it. It is lifted up on to a lampstand for all to see. Now the one who is our light is lifted up on to the lampstand of the cross for all sufferers to see better in the darkness of their pain. From this cross he looks at us in our sickness and pain and says, 'You are not alone. I am with you and I understand. You and I together can cope. We can bring the light of love into this darkness. We can bring some meaning into this otherwise meaningless experience. You can share with me not only in my suffering, but in my saving of the world through my sacrifice.' We are not talking here of merely putting up with what cannot be avoided or of making the best of a bad situation. We are talking of a great mystery, of a new life, a deeper, fuller life hidden with Christ in God. And the source of that life is that figure on the cross. In this suffering he says to us, 'Learn from me and my suffering that our suffering, yours and mine, does not mean that our Father is not aware of us or that he does not care. No, he is closer than ever before. Let us both surrender ourselves into his love. He will deliver us.'

This suffering of our Saviour, borne with such love for us, has inspired his followers of all ages to heroic patience and love in times of suffering, sickness and pain. A Protestant pastor describes his imprisonment and torture in a former communist country in Eastern Europe. One day, having been savagely beaten, especially on the face, he was brought before the commanding officer for questioning. He was asked, 'Do you still insist that you are made in the image and likeness of God?' When he said yes, the officer produced a mirror, showed him his mutilated face and said mockingly, 'Then your God must be very ugly.' The pastor answered that God had many faces and one of those faces was worn by Jesus on the cross; it was the face foretold by Isaiah: 'The crowds were appalled on seeing him, so disfigured did he look that he seemed no longer human' (Is 52:14). The pastor said he was confident that Jesus would recognise him as his brother.

When we say that the suffering Christ brings us new wisdom and power in our sickness, we are not saying that all the storms become calm in our spirit. Questioning and complaint will still surface, along with the desire to escape, to find a short-cut, to jump over the sickness and pain. We need not be ashamed of this. It is part of our human condition. The Christ we are contemplating also experienced this. In the garden of Gethsemane, when he was overwhelmed by sadness, fear and loneliness, he cries out against his situation. He wants to jump over what is coming. 'My Father, if it is possible, let this cup pass me by' (Mt 26:39). But his Father asks him to go through. Again, on Calvary, the crowd want him to take the short-cut. 'Let the Christ, the King of Israel, come down from the cross now for us to see it and believe' (Mk 15:32). They tempt him, 'Come down. There is no need to suffer. If you are God, come down and show

70

us that you are master over pain and suffering and we will believe.' But Jesus proves his true mastery over pain and suffering by staying there and overcoming it.

The poet Robert Frost says that 'the best way out is always through'. This passion and death will inspire many to follow Jesus through suffering. Paul writes to the Romans about these people. He lists their trials and sufferings and says it is precisely through their endurance that they have the victory. 'Nothing therefore can come between us and the love of Christ, even if we are troubled or worried, or being persecuted, or lacking food or clothes or being threatened or even attacked. These are the trials through which we triumph by the power of him who loved us' (Rm 8:35-37).

One of the most painful aspects of serious sickness is the loss of control over our own destinies. Some people are sickly or handicapped from early years. Some are struck in later years by unexpected sickness which confines them to hospital or bed for months, maybe years. Others are suddenly disabled, even paralysed, by an accident. Gradually, or maybe suddenly, people are cut off from normal activity, from any possibility of achievement. Life seems to lose meaning and purpose. The control of their lives passes into the hands of others. They become dependent on health workers, family and friends. There is a sense of powerlessness. In *The Good Friday People* Sheila Cassidy writes about people in different countries who struggle against the injustices of our world. She says they are ordinary weak people like us who felt the call to walk with Christ to Jerusalem to oppose injustice. In their powerlessness, the mystery of the Risen Lord always breaks through. She offers this moving insight: 'Powerlessness is a sacrament, an outward sign of an inward truth, that we are totally dependent on the God who made us.' This word surely applies to this present reflection. The powerlessness of the sick need not be an empty, wasted experience. It can be a kind of sacrament, an outward sign of new inner power, of a new experience of God's power in our weakness.

Sickness can lead to a new discovery of that deepest truth, that my life is always in God's hands. Many sick people cannot organise their own lives and are dependent on others, but in a deeper sense they are dependent on God. Ultimately their lives are in the hands of God as the life of Jesus was in his passion and death. Jesus too had lost all control over his life from the moment of his arrest in the garden. There he is taken and brought to Annas, who sends him to Caiaphas, who hands him over to Pilate, who passes him on to Herod, who returns him to Pilate, who finally hands him to the soldiers. He is completely in the hands of others who can do with him as they please. But in his heart Jesus had surrendered himself to a loving Father in whom he never ceased to trust. The crowd mocked him for this and knew of only one kind of deliverance, the escape, the last-minute rescue. 'He put his trust in God; now let God rescue him' (Mt 27:43). But Jesus does not lose trust. He is ready to go through his passion and death, holding his Father's hand. Thus he saves our world and invites us in our sickness to join him in this act of salvation. He asks us to allow our powerlessness to be the sacrament of his power. He asks us in union with him to tap into that deep current of life-giving water, the sustaining love of his Father. Then, in a dark and mysterious way, we will have some experience of that fullness of life he came to bring.

All the time of our sickness, our poor bodies suffer their own passion. They endure the humiliation of weakness and pain, the fevers and nausea, the vomiting and wasting diarrhoea, the pains of cancer, AIDS, migraine, shingles, arthritis. All this dulls the spirit and we cannot pray. We can only endure. I suggest a reflection here out of personal experience. It will not take away pain but may help to bring some interior peace. Some years ago I had a severe attack of malaria. Unable to hold down any medicine, I could not shake off the high temperature. I felt very sorry for myself and had that dark thought, 'will I ever be right again!' I also felt angry with my body. I was blaming it for being so weak, for bringing me pain, for not responding to medicine. Then suddenly I realised how terribly unjust I was to my body. That was a moment of grace for me. It was as if my body spoke up and reminded me that it had been my friend and companion all through life. It had taken me everywhere. It was the instrument that had brought me knowledge and all my experience of life and of so much beauty and happiness. It had taken some bad knocks in sickness and accident. It did not enjoy vomiting or headaches but it never gave in and always rallied. It had accompanied me on my journey to God in prayer. It complained now about an earlier foolish spirituality which taught me to see it as an enemy of the spirit, an enemy of prayer, when in fact it really wanted to join my spirit in worship and praise. It had been anointed with holy oil in sacraments and it is destined for immortality.

I realised I had truly sinned against my body. I had broken St

Paul's word, 'No one hates his own body' (Ep 5:29). I apologised and was reconciled with my body. Then my body asked me to look at my Saviour on the cross and consider his body. Did he hate his body for carrying the pain in his wounded hands and feet? He had taken his body with great love from Mary in the incarnation and in doing so told me that the body is good and beautiful. After Calvary, the women will look for his body to anoint it with respect. But it won't be necessary. His Father had received it into his hands and anointed it with love and raised it into glory, and Jesus will proudly show off the wounds it still carries. If our bodies can share in praise and worship, they can share in this special worship of surrender which sickness asks of us. The body can do so more patiently and peacefully when it is recognised and loved for what it really is, an old and dear friend. On the surface, sickness is a diminishing of life, but at a deeper, more hidden level, it is a sharing of the life of our Saviour who suffers and dies out of love for the world.

When Jesus began his agony in Gethsemane we are told that a great sadness and distress came over him. Then he said to them, 'My soul is sorrowful to the point of death. Wait here and keep awake with me' (Mt 26:37). Jesus, who had earlier claimed that he was never alone because his Father was always with him, is now so humanly distressed that he needs human companionship. He does not ask his three friends to do anything, but simply to be there. He needs them near him. In humbly, patiently bearing our share of sickness and suffering, we can be near him in a real sense. We can offer him our companionship as we cope with our own distress. We don't have to do anything, just be with him. In this way our sickness and pain need not be wasted but can be a kind of sacrament, an outward sign of our true inner love for him and of our union with him in his act of saving and healing the world.

73

16

NO SUCH PLACE AS DEATH

'Pilate, astonished that Jesus should have died so soon, summoned the centurion and enquired if he was already dead. Having been assured of this by the centurion, he granted the corpse to Joseph, who bought a shroud, took Jesus down from the cross, wrapped him in the shroud and laid him in a tomb which had been hewn out of the rock' (Mk 15:44-46).

It was a simple funeral. So Jesus shares all with us: life, death, funeral, grave. We have been saying that the lives of most people are hidden and unnoticed. If this is true of our lives, it is even more true of our deaths. No matter what the circumstances of death, it is surely for each of us our most hidden experience. Whether we die young or old, alone or with friends, suddenly or gradually, the experience of passing through death to the world beyond is completely personal to us and is the most hidden part of our lives. Even here, into this most hidden place, Jesus enters. He does so out of love for us, to light the way and assure us it is safe to follow. We say we die alone, but again, the deeper reality is hidden, we die with Christ. If Paul can say to us who believe in Jesus, 'The life you have is hidden with Christ in God,' we can now say with courage, hope and joy, 'The death we die is hidden with Christ in God.'

It is in the moment of death, this moment of deepest mystery, that all externals are finally stripped away. We are left with the essential, the hidden life we have been speaking about. In the moment of death we will see its beauty clearly for the first time and will realise that only this is real and, what is even more wonderful, that this hidden life of love with God does not die. It does not die because God and love are forever. Jesus came to give us life in its fullness. It is in death that we experience that richness and fullness. This may throw some light on those strange words Jesus spoke to Martha after the death of her brother Lazarus: 'If anyone believes in me, even though he dies he will live, and whoever lives and believes in me will never die. We will never die because true love never dies. God is love. We are made in his image. The truest expression of life is love and we are made to love. I do not say that we succeed. In fact, we often fail. We love imperfectly and selfishly. But still, deep inside, we know that the most worthwhile thing we can do on this earth is to try to go out to others in love.

Paul says, 'Love does not come to an end' (I Co 13:8). We sense that this must be so despite our human failure in loving. We sense it because we cannot ignore our very being which is made in the image of God who is love. We could not imagine a mother saying to her baby, 'I will love you till you are fifteen and then you can manage for yourself!' It would be a strange lover who could say to his beloved, 'I will love you with all my heart for the next five years and we can then review the situation.' It has been said, 'When a person says to you "I love you", he is saying "You will not die".' God, in creating us and sharing his life with us, was saying 'I love you.' Jesus, in dying for us on Calvary, was saying 'I love you'. It was just another way of saying 'You will not die'.

The burial of Jesus that Friday evening was rushed because the Sabbath was about to begin. On Sunday morning his friends come to the tomb to complete the anointing of his body. They are met by heavenly messengers who speak strange words: 'Why look among the dead for someone who is alive?' (Lk 24:5). Again we are invited to look for reality beneath the externals and are even forced to ask what we mean by death. The messengers say that Jesus is living. He has not passed from life to a place or state called death. He has passed from this life through death into fullness of life. His hidden life of love for his Father did not die. He simply surrendered himself into his Father's arms. For Jesus, death is not a movement to any dark, cold, lifeless place. There is no such 'place'.

Jesus does not see death as a place or condition, some kind of reality out there where people go and wait for some time or all time. On earth we have our graves and urns and graveyards, but these are not inhabited. When the sharp edge of grief wears off, we visit these places and pray. They are links, places of memory, but our loved ones are not there. Nor are they in some kind of celestial cemetery. They are in a new and beautiful life hidden with Christ in God.

For Jesus there is only and always life and love. Life, the gift of love, once given, is never taken back. It is only changed into a fullness of wonder and beauty. I am consoled by the miracle of a seed. If a small, dry, shrivelled seed can 'become' a flower with all its beauty of form, colour and perfume, then I feel I can confidently leave my own transformation in the hands of that God whom Jesus called a gardener. Life is given in love by God, who does not take back his gifts.

When we were children, we had an angry little verse we would use against each other, if one of us in childish upset tried to take back a present he had given to the other. It went like this:

> Give a thing, take it back – God will ask you where's that. If you say you don't know – he will send you down below.

The verse was terrible and the childish theology fearsome but the intuition was good; a gift given should not be taken back. God does not take back the gift of life and so Jesus speaks of never dying.

One day Jesus was confronted by a group called the Sadducees. These people did not believe in resurrection and were challenging Jesus. In his reply Jesus used a simple argument. He pointed out that in scripture, Yahweh is called the God of Abraham, Isaac and Jacob. But if there is no resurrection these great ancestors are dead and have no existence. Surely it would be ridiculous to be called the God of persons who did not exist; it would be a meaningless title. Therefore, these ancestors must be alive. 'Moses himself implies that the dead rise again, in the passage about the bush when he calls the Lord the God of Abraham, the God of Isaac and the God of Jacob. Now he is God, not of the dead, but of the living; for to him in fact all men are alive' (Lk 20:37-38). Jesus says that in God's eyes all are alive. We can see from the gospels that he also looked at death in the same way as his Father. The gospels record three incidents when Jesus raised a person from the dead. The interesting thing to notice is that on each occasion Jesus speaks directly to the dead person. He does not speak to his Father to intercede for the person. He looks into the face of death and speaks directly to the person, knowing he will be heard. To the daughter of Jairus the synagogue official he says, 'Little girl, I tell you to get up' (Mk 5:41). To the only son of the widow of Nain he says, 'Young man, I tell you to get up' (Lk 7:15), and to his friend Lazarus, the brother of Martha and Mary, he cries out in a loud voice, 'Lazarus, here! Come out!' (Jn 11:43).

For Jesus there is no such reality as a dead person. As with his Father, to him all are alive. But even still he shares our human grief in mourning. He is always moved by the suffering of the mourners. He was not even asked to help the widow's son but Luke tells us, 'When the Lord saw her he felt sorry for her. "Do not cry," he said' (Lk 7:13). He himself openly weeps for Martha and Mary in their loss of Lazarus. On all these occasions Jesus, having raised the person, then rejoices with those whose mourning is turned to joy. He rejoices in the family reunion, in the human love that binds together all those involved. For God, resurrection means reunion with loved ones, just as for Jesus himself, it meant union with his Father. We see this loving sensitivity in a most beautiful human gesture after the raising of the widow's son. 'And the dead man sat up and began to talk, and Jesus gave him to his mother' (Lk 7:18). Jesus had felt sorry for the woman. He now gives the boy back to his mother and rejoices in their reunion. This same Jesus will one day give back every son and daughter to their mothers and fathers and reunite all separated lovers.

Here let us consider for a moment one of the sharper griefs of certain mourners. I think of the grief of people mourning for a loved one who dies in especially tragic circumstances. I think, for example, of parents who mourn for a son or daughter who committed suicide, of a mother mourning a daughter who dies while having an abortion, of a father grieving for a son who died from an overdose of drugs. I think of a wife mourning her husband who abandoned her and then gave up his faith and died without prayer; of someone watching a friend die full of anger, unable to forgive another person or to forgive God for unhappiness in life; of parents grieving for a son who joined a terrorist group and was blown up by the bomb he was carrying to kill others. The grief in all these cases has a very sharp edge. It is grief not only for this present separation and loneliness. There is the more terrible, desperate fear of the possibility of eternal separation. Can the Jesus who gave back the young man of Nain to his mother give back these loved ones to one another in the resurrection?

I am certain that the Jesus who gave back the daughter to Jairus and changed the mourning of that house to dancing, the Jesus who reunited the young man of Nain and his mother and who rejoiced in the reunion of Lazarus with Martha and Mary, this same Jesus can and will in the resurrection reunite those loved ones involved in the kind of tragic deaths we mention. Jesus was present in all those situations, present not as judge but as compassionate, healing love, present as Saviour. For Jesus there is no such thing as a hopeless case. When he was on his way to the house of Jairus to heal his daughter, he was delayed by a woman looking for healing. During this interruption and delay messengers came with the news that the little girl had died. They said, 'Your daughter is dead: why put the master to any further trouble?' (Mk 5:35). It seemed a hopeless case. The girl is dead, why pray or ask any more. But the gospel continues, 'But Jesus had overheard this remark of theirs and he said to the official, 'Do not be afraid; only have faith' (Mk 5:36).

And so, to the people involved in the kind of tragedies we mentioned, Jesus says exactly the same: 'Please don't be afraid, only have faith.' You see, he is Love, and nothing is impossible to Love. His healing love is a deep current flowing all the time underneath all the ugly surface appearances of hate, anger, frustration, violence and fear in the lives of those involved. His love is infinitely greater than our weakness. Jesus overhears us saying to one another, 'Why bother God about that case; it's hopeless.' Again he says, 'I told you, don't be afraid, have faith, pray in peace.' Those who mourn in such circumstances could make for their loved ones Jesus' own dying prayer, 'Father, into your hands we commend their spirits. We place their troubled spirits in your loving hands. Receive into your gentle, healing hands our son, daughter, wife, husband, friend who died in such a way. We know that you receive them and that in your hands they are safe and at peace.' Make that prayer with faith and love and be at peace. Our heavenly Father will not be outdone in love by us, his children.

Let us stop trying to imagine the love of God as something 'out there' which we can look at and maybe measure. It is the very Mystery of God himself, his very Being. About him revelation does not say, 'God *has* love' but 'God *is* Love' (I Jn 4:8). In him who is Love we live and move and have our being (Ac 17:28). That love surrounds us as the water surrounds the fish in the sea. Let us stop trying to understand what is beyond our understanding (Ep 3:19). Let us become as children and surrender joyfully to that love which embraces us all. Let us go beyond appearances and get in touch with that hidden life we have been speaking of, that life hidden with Christ in God who is Love.

17

WHO IS IN CHARGE?

'Why look among the dead for someone who is alive? He is not here; he has risen' (Lk 24:5). When our story of Jesus moves past the tomb to reveal his new and risen life, it takes us into a land where we are total strangers. Jesus passes into glory. Here we are without any experience. Despite this we have preconceived ideas of what God and glory might be like. Jesus, who came to reveal the true God, continually surprises us. Let us humble ourselves again and allow him to teach us. I have always been grateful for the closing chapters of the gospels which show us the Risen Lord. If the story of Jesus had ended with his burial and we had no account of the apparitions, how might we have imagined Jesus in his risen life? For us glory means a great brightness impossible to hide, totally other-worldly and awe-inspiring. We might have imagined something like the transfiguration scene when Peter and his companions could not look at the Lord in his brightness and had to bow their faces to the ground. Fortunately we are not left to our imaginations. How, in fact do the gospel writers present the risen Lord? They show a man moving about in the early morning in a garden, a man so ordinary he is mistaken for the gardener. They describe three men strolling along a country road – one of the three is the risen Lord. They show a young man lighting a fire by the lakeside and greeting fishermen coming in from a night's fishing. This is Jesus, risen Lord, passed over into glory.

God always surprises us. When Jesus passed from the hidden life of Nazareth to his public life, we expected drama and power, but God will not accept our scenario. That which gives meaning, beauty and value to life still remains hidden. Now he passes into glory and we expect dramatic change, but he is the same Jesus, gentle, compassionate, approachable and forgiving. He is glory, yes. But he is love and that is the real glory, the hidden glory in him and ourselves. Again, in the risen life, he is asking us to look past externals and realise the wonder, beauty and meaning that are already within us. That is the good news he continues to share with us now in his glory. This Lord we see in the resurrection stories is Jesus as he is now today, the Jesus we meet in prayer, in sacrament, in scripture and in one another.

Let us look at one resurrection story in some detail. It is the story of two discouraged and frightened disciples who left Jerusalem that Sunday morning after the Sabbath rest. They set out for a village called Emmaus with only one wish, to get away from Jerusalem, the place of danger and broken dreams. The risen Lord joins them on the road. Luke, in chapter 24 of his gospel, tells us much about the meaning of the resurrection and how the same risen Lord will meet us today and interact with us, especially in prayer. First let us notice that in this meeting Jesus takes the initiative and joins the two men. We so easily take this for granted. We should not. Recall the background. On Thursday night Jesus had been arrested, unjustly condemned and handed over to a foreign government for execution. His frightened and confused followers ran away. The death of Jesus was the death of all their dreams. Now as these two slip away from Jerusalem, they are still trying to understand what had gone wrong. 'Now as they talked this over, Jesus himself came up and walked by their side but something prevented them from recognising him' (Lk 24:15-16).

Jesus joins them and walks with them, not because they had been faithful, not because they had trusted him and stood by him. They had done none of these things. He joins them because they were weak, afraid, guilty and confused. On our walk through life, we will hit bad patches when darkness, doubt, fear and guilt overcome us, when our dreams come crashing down around us and we have no answers. We just want to walk away from it all. These are the times when we will least feel like praying. We will have no feeling of faith, no desire for spiritual things. Things may be so bad that we feel there is no God, no Jesus. He is dead and buried as far as we are concerned. It is then that we need him most and it is then that he is most ready to be with us, even if we don't recognise him, even if all we have to say is something like what these men said to him, that they knew he had died and was buried, but the story that he had risen was only the rumour of certain women. But just give him a chance. These two men were at least talking about him and recalling his story. Take your scripture, recall the story and he will join you on the way.

Jesus joins the two disciples and walks with them at their pace and in their direction. They are heading away from Jerusalem towards Emmaus. Now Jesus wants them back in Jerusalem where there is work for them to do. But he does not stop them and try to turn them around. They are not yet ready to go back. When they are ready, they will go back joyfully. So Jesus walks with them to Emmaus. It may take us a long time in life to find the right direction, to know where the Lord wants us to go. Meanwhile he is gentle and patient. He won't hassle or bully us and all the while he will walk with us. These two men will eventually turn around and head back, but only after they have looked into the face of Jesus and recognised him. Then, in recognising that it really is Jesus, they will realise that he still loves them and forgives all. They will recognise him as he breaks bread with them. That moment will be a moment of awareness of being loved and totally accepted. This will be their conversion. Now they can turn around joyfully and run back to Jerusalem.

On this walk Jesus asks these men what they are talking about and why they are sad. In prayer he will ask us the same. He wants us to share our hearts with him. He wants to hear our stories, the things going on deep within us. It does not matter if we have got things all wrong as these two friends had. He wants to know what upsets us. Later he will give us his side of the stories but first he wants to hear our side. We must be totally honest in expressing our fears, anger, doubts and disappointment. Jesus can cope. These two tell him all about their friend Jesus and all the dreams they had built around him. Then came his betrayal, weakness, death, the end. When they have finished, Jesus takes up the very same story and gently leads them into a new understanding of these very same events.

In their eyes the events were accidents, mistakes, disasters caused by evil people. Now Jesus uncovers a deeper reality hiding under those events. He opens their eyes to God present and at work in all that had happened, to a loving God at work bringing good out of evil, love out of hate, a God never overcome by evil but overcoming evil with love. What they saw as mistake, accident and tragedy was under God's control. Now, as they see this hidden reality with God's eyes, their hearts begin to burn within them.

Let us ask why these two men left Jerusalem that Sunday morning. They left because things had not turned out the way they had expected. But things had turned out the way God expected. They left Jerusalem because they had dreams which were now shattered. But God also had dreams and these were now being fulfilled, dreams more wonderful than their small minds could imagine. They had dreams for Israel. God had dreams for all people. They dreamed of political and economic greatness but God's dreams touched the deepest, most real, lasting part of each of us. The mistake of these men was not that they dreamed dreams, but that their dreams were so small and poor. We are lucky that God does not confine himself to our dreams. And often this God may have to turn our small dreamworld upside down so that his dreams of wonder and beauty for us may be realised in our lives.

In the eyes of these two men Jesus and God had lost control of events on that Thursday night in Gethsemane. Caiaphas and Pilate had taken over and were deciding the world's destiny by destroying the Messiah. Now the Resurrection contradicts all this. The risen Lord assures his friends that God had not lost control. Through all this suffering, rejection, hatred and violence, through this apparently horrible failure, God's saving plan was working out, like a seed breaking up in the dark earth ready to send out a fresh green shoot of new life and beauty. God is always present and at work in hidden, loving ways, even in the most painful or evil situation. His love is always stronger than evil. His providence cannot be frustrated. It is interesting to notice how we use the word 'providence' in daily speech. We use it only when good things happen. We say that 'it was providential you were late for that bus which crashed'. We thus suggest that providence was not at work for those who did travel and died in the crash. We just don't think of God as present and loving when bad things happen and things go wrong or do not turn out as we hoped. We seem to imagine then that God has left us and that we are on our own.

The passion, death and Resurrection of Jesus totally contradict this assumption and challenge us to accept a new and much richer understanding of Providence, that God is present in all situations and is even closer than ever in a specially active and loving way when things, as we say, go all wrong. This is the Good News. It was the realisation of this that was growing in the hearts of the two men on the Emmaus road. Jesus did not tell them he had 'escaped' death, or that he had managed to survive, or that things had not been as bad as they had imagined. He offered no such easy comfort. That would not really be good news. The real and most wonderful good news was that he had gone through the worst that could happen and had overcome the worst imaginable evil with love and was now raised to new life, where they were to follow if they would walk the same path of love. And because it is not an easy path, he is still with them, sharing his love and power with them. This was the good news that transformed these men and sent them racing back to Jerusalem.

This was the good news that enabled the early followers of Jesus, simple men and women, to challenge the power of the mighty Roman Empire. There is a beautiful illustration of this vibrant faith in God's providence and the presence of the risen Lord among those early believers in a second-century document recording the martyrdom of St Polycarp in 155 AD. Here is the record:

> It was the second day of the first fortnight of Xanthicus, seven days before the Kalends of March, when our blessed Polycarp died his martyr's death two hours before midday on the Greater Sabbath. The official responsible for his arrest was Herod; the High Priest was Philip of Tralles; and the Proconsul was Statius Quadratus – but the ruling monarch was Jesus Christ, who reigns forever and ever. To him be ascribed all glory, honour, majesty and an eternal throne from generation to generation. Amen.

These early Christians had no doubt about who was really in charge!

The Emmaus story has a beautiful ending. As the three men approach the village, Jesus pretends to go on, and of course his friends press him to stay. 'They pressed him to stay with them. "It is nearly evening," they said, "and the day is almost over".' So he went in to stay with them' (Lk 24:29-30). He shares their meal and they recognise him in the breaking of the bread. Then he vanishes from their sight. I used to be puzzled by their reaction to his disappearance. I would have expected them to be disappointed, to feel lonely, to sit and feel sorry and wish he had stayed. But there is no such reaction. They race off to Jerusalem full of joy. And here is the very heart of the meaning of Jesus and all I have been saying here. The reaction of these men was totally correct because their new joy remains. It is an experience of the heart, of love, not dependent on any visible, tangible presence of Jesus. They have a new inner life. They are a new creation in Christ. This is the hidden life we are speaking of. It is love, joy, power. It enables them to do what was impossible before, to return to Jerusalem, the city of broken dreams. It empowers them now to do with joy what before was a burden. Even though it is late in the day, they set out 'that instant', their hearts burning within them. They do not leave Jesus in Emmaus. They do not leave Jesus anywhere any more. He is with them in their hearts. Their truest life is hidden with him in God.

Tell me, is he hidden in your heart too?

18

HEALED ON THE WAY

When Jesus and the two disciples reached Emmaus, he made as if to go on, but his friends invited him to stay with them. He had joined them on the road. But now he leaves them free. He will not impose himself on them and he moves to go on. Happily they invite him to stay. He accepts, shares their meal and they recognise him. Then, even when he vanishes, they are full of a new life and joy and are ready to return to Jerusalem. They had invited Jesus to enter their house and he had entered their hearts. We say this Emmaus experience is a good image of prayer. Because of our baptism, all of us in our Christian lives are in some way walking with Jesus. But perhaps we have not really recognised him, nor appreciated the beauty and power of his friendship. Now we must do something more. He will not impose himself on us. We must invite him to stay with us in prayer.

Often our desire for a better understanding of the Lord comes at a crisis point of life when dreams have been shattered, when life loses meaning and we are at rock bottom, just as the Emmaus disciples were. At this point our hearts may whisper, 'Stay with me, Lord. I am lost'. This is a desire for prayer. I am not thinking here of our vocal prayers and traditional devotions. I speak of what is commonly called contemplation, when we become still and, with the help of the Holy Spirit, become aware of the indwelling of God. In such prayer the gaze of our hearts rests on the Lord and we listen and he speaks to us through scripture or through the events of our lives as he spoke to those two men. He will help us see the deeper meaning of what is going on in our lives and how God is lovingly present even in the more painful and confusing events. This closer walk with Jesus is a life-giving but hidden experience. Our life of prayer is hidden with Christ in God.

Prayer is a hidden experience chiefly because it is a faith experience. 'Only faith can prove the existence of the realities that at present remain unseen' (Heb 11:1). Faith and prayer touch the unseen, hidden reality. Prayer is a supreme act of trust in the reality of a power infinitely greater than ourselves, the power of love which is the source of all healing, growth and life. Paul says

Jesus is that love made visible (Rm 8:39). That does not mean that everyone who met Jesus in the flesh saw God's glory and surrendered to his love. We know that people responded very differently to Jesus and many rejected him. Faith is always needed to 'see', touch and experience the deep healing power of God hiding in Jesus. Many did respond to Jesus in faith. They were always people in some need who could admit that need and trusted that Jesus could help them. Such people experienced a healing, saving, transforming power in their meetings with Jesus. The basic ingredients of this faith are a humble admission that I need help, a trust that Jesus can give that help and a willingness to ask for it.

Some gospel stories describe faith encounters between Jesus and certain people who experienced his saving power in their lives. I draw attention to a simple overall pattern I have noticed in many of these stories and I believe that this can help us in our reflection on prayer. The first example is the miracle of the changing of water to wine at Cana. The wine at the wedding feast has run out. Mary informs Jesus and then tells the servants to do whatever her son tells them. Jesus instructs the servants to fill the large ablution jars with water and then to draw from the jars and bring the drink to the master of ceremonies. They do so and the water has become a fine wine. I ask you to notice three elements in this incident which are repeated in many other miracle stories. Firstly, what Jesus asks from those in need is something very simple, completely within their power: 'Fill the jars with water' (Jn 2:7). Secondly, what he asks seems in some way futile, even foolish, in view of the need. 'Draw out water and bring it to the MC.' Finally, the outcome is a blessing out of all proportion to the contribution made by those in need – a very large supply of superior quality wine is provided for the guests.

Consider some other examples. A very large crowd has followed Jesus out into the desert to listen to him. It is evening and Jesus, concerned about their hunger, suggests feeding them. The disciples say they have only five loaves and two fish. Jesus asks them to do something very easy, to offer their small amount of food. Then he asks them to do something quite futile, to begin distributing this small amount to the great crowd (Mt 14:19). When the disciples cooperate, the crowd is fed and satisfied. One day Jesus sees a blind man. He makes a paste of clay and spittle and tells the man to go to the Pool of Siloam and wash (Jn 9:7). An easy

86

task, but apparently foolish. The man washes his eyes in the pool and he can see. Jesus arrives at the village of Bethany too late to save his friend Lazarus. He asks Mary and Martha to take him to the tomb and then gives the strange command to roll back the stone from the entrance to the tomb (Jn 11:39). The sisters protest that Lazarus has been buried for four days. Jesus repeats his request, so easy but so futile, to remove the stone. When they make that simple contribution Lazarus is raised.

One day, as Jesus enters a village, ten lepers approach him asking for healing. Jesus hears their cry and makes a strange response. He says,'Go and show yourselves to the priests' (Lk 17:14). This was the same as saying 'You are healed.' Lepers were forbidden to mix in society for fear of infecting others. If a leper was cured he had to show himself to the priests and get a certificate guaranteeing the cure and allowing him to mix with people. These ten lepers must have wondered at this directive from Jesus as they looked at their deformed limbs and knew that they were not cured. But they don't protest. They follow the simple but seemingly futile order and set out to find the priests and they are healed on the way. 'Now as they were going away they were cleansed' (Lk 17:15). This last story illustrates very powerfully the dynamic at work in all faith activity, that the power released by faith is experienced in the doing, in the surrender to God's invitation. These lepers are cured while they are on the way. This is true of the faith exercise we call prayer. We will experience God's power in prayer not by reading books or attending seminars on prayer but by giving time to prayer.

Consider one more example. Peter and his friends have spent a whole night on the lake fishing and have caught nothing. Jesus meets them on the shore in the morning and asks to use their boat while teaching the crowd on the shore. After teaching for some time Jesus asks Peter to put out the nets for a catch of fish. Peter reminds Jesus that he has fished all night and caught nothing. But he does what he is asked and nets a great haul of fish. Notice what Peter says when he agrees to put out the nets. 'We worked hard all night long and caught nothing, but if you say so, I will put out the nets' (Lk 5:5). This is the mainspring of faith and of prayer. It is a response to a word from God. 'If you say so.' God takes the initiative and we respond to that hidden dimension in every life situation, the reality of God present, actively healing and re-creating.

In prayer that healing love is touched and power is released. The pattern of rewarded faith in these gospel stories says something about prayer. Prayer asks something easy of us, something completely within our power, to spend some quiet time with God. But this activity seems to many to be futile, even a waste of time. However, those who respond in faith and persevere will experience God's power at work in them, blessing them out of all proportion to the effort they put into prayer. And if you are tempted to make the excuse that you are not worthy, then let us go back for a moment to that last scene of Peter and his catch of fish. We see Peter with a boat full of fish which must have gladdened his fisherman's heart. But there is a deeper, more wonderful joy in store for him, a joy similar to that experienced by the Emmaus disciples. When Peter sees the miracle of the catch of fish and realises he is in the presence of someone close to God, he becomes sharply aware of his own unworthiness and in confusion throws himself at the feet of Jesus saying, 'Leave me Lord, I am a sinful man' (Lk 5:8). You and I can understand what is going on in his heart. Then Peter hears words of gentle assurance telling him not to be afraid and inviting him to an even closer companionship and to work with the Lord in sharing the good news. Jesus is telling Peter that he is known, accepted and loved as he is in all his weakness. The Emmaus disciples had failed Jesus in every possible way by their fear and lack of faith and yet Jesus wanted to be with them and wanted them to invite him home. We are no better than Peter or those men. And we are no less loved. We may feel totally unworthy of the close friendship of Jesus in prayer. That has nothing to do with it. He wants to be close to us as we are. Will we invite him home in prayer?

In prayer we meet Jesus, but it is a faith meeting, as it was for the people in those gospel stories. In gospel days, many people met Jesus but did not touch him at the deeper level of faith. One day, a large crowd pressed around Jesus on his way to the house of Jairus. They hoped to see a miracle. They jostled against him and touched him. One woman in the crowd touched the hem of his garment with faith and was healed. Jesus stopped and asked, 'Who touched me?' The disciples said, 'You see how the crowd is pressing round you and yet you say, "Who touched me?" (Mk 5:31). Many people touched Jesus that day. Only one touched him with faith. We can meet and touch Jesus in prayer but we must approach him with faith.

St Paul, writing to the early Christians who had not met Jesus in the flesh, says that they too can meet him in faith and experience his power. He also says that even the very first followers, who had actually met Jesus in the flesh, now know him in a faith way in his risen and glorified state. He writes, 'Even if we did once know Christ in the flesh, that is not how we know him now. And for anyone who is in Christ, there is a new creation; the old creation has gone, and now the new one is here' (II Co 5:16-18). Notice the strong expression Paul uses to describe the transformation that can take place when we meet and recognise the risen Lord. He says we become 'a new creation'. We think of the Emmaus disciples. They are transformed men as they run back to Jerusalem. It's not a question of having a new outlook, a new insight, a new philosophy. They simply have a new life, new power. Jesus offers us nothing less, and it is his own hidden life of love.

Jesus is the vine, we are the branches. We must abide in him in prayer that this hidden life will be continuously nourished, grow and be fruitful. In this prayer we are asked for a small contribution. Usually that is all we can manage: fill the jars, bring your five loaves, wash in the pool, roll back the stone, cast your nets, be still for half an hour. Let us respond in joyful, humble faith and discover 'him whose power, working in us, can do infinitely more than we can ask or imagine' (Ep 3:20).

19

WE CANNOT BYPASS TIME

We have looked at several stories of people in need who came to Jesus for help. In each case he asked them to do something as a sign of their faith. What he asked was always something very small and in each case their small act of cooperation was rewarded with great blessings. Let us look at a similar beautiful story in the Old Testament, told in the Second Book of Kings. Naaman, army commander to the King of Aram, is a leper. In his house there is a young Jewish girl captured as a slave during a raid on Israel. This girl tells Naaman's wife that her husband could be cured of his leprosy by one of Israel's prophets. The King loves Naaman and so sends him to Israel with rich gifts to ask for a cure. The King of Israel receives the envoys in great distress for he knows he cannot cure leprosy. He fears he is being provoked into war. Elisha the prophet hears of the King's distress and tells him to send Naaman to him.

When Naaman presents himself to Elisha, the prophet simply tells him to go and wash seven times in the Jordan. Naaman is indignant and says the rivers back home are as good as the Jordan. He prepares to leave in anger. But his servants are wiser and say to him, 'My father, if the prophet had asked you to do something difficult, would you not have done it? All the more reason, then, when he says to you, bathe and you will become clean' (II K 5:13). Naaman follows the good advice, bathes in the Jordan and is cured. Again I think of the faith exercise of prayer. We are asked for a small simple contribution. Maybe like Naaman we are humbled. Like him, maybe we expect to be asked to do something more difficult, more exciting. What we are asked for in prayer is something simple and humble, to spend some time each day in silence with the Lord.

If prayer asks for something completely within our power, why do more people not give prayer a chance? I suppose to many it seems like a waste of time to sit alone in silence for half an hour or more. It seems a kind of foolishness, like serving water to wedding guests, or starting to cut up five loaves to feed a great crowd, or washing in the local river to be cured of leprosy! We must repeat, prayer is not a human skill but is essentially a faith exercise. It is a faith response; someone else has spoken first. We only respond to an invitation from God. One of the first things this faith tells me is that I am never alone, that at each moment God breathes life into me in love. I have to become still to become aware of this God who is nearer to me than I am to myself.

The silence and stillness of prayer is not an empty waiting for something to happen. Nor do I have to make anything happen. I become still to become aware of the miracle happening all the time, God wanting me and loving me into life. 'Awareness' is a good word in helping us understand prayer. It suggests that something is happening, some activity is going on which I did not initiate. My part is to stop, notice, become aware and allow the awareness to touch me. I stop, just as I might stop on a walk to admire something beautiful – a tree, a flower, a rainbow, a bird singing. I stop, notice, accept, rejoice. This beauty is gift. In prayer I stop to notice, admire and rejoice in the giver of all beauty. St Augustine says, 'I sought you outside of me, but all the while you were within.' And again he says, 'You were with me, but I was not with you.' Prayer is becoming aware of this indwelling God and seeking to be with him.

Awareness suggests wonder and mystery. It suggests that someone else is active before I begin to pray. At no moment am I alone. Each moment the ever-present active God is loving me. Prayer invites me to taste and relish what I so often miss, the richness of the present moment. Each moment of life, each breath is a gift. Prayer invites me to notice and accept this, to sink down into the present moment, deep down past all accidentals, all shadows, all externals, down to its source, roots and origin, which is the love of God. 'If I can only touch the hem of his garment, I shall be well again.' So said that woman of faith in the gospel. The present moment invites me to such an act of faith, to touch God present to me in this still moment of prayer.

'Awareness' is only a threshold word, an introductory word. It introduces us to hidden reality, to our roots, to the deep spring of living water promised by Jesus (Jn 7:37). In touch with our roots and with this living water, we can grow like the tree planted by running water. Prayer deals with life and therefore with growth. The life we speak of is that hidden life we share with Jesus, our personal relationship of love with God. The deepest and most meaningful development throughout our lives will be the growth of this relationship. Now, growth takes time and here we have a problem. We are not good at waiting. We live in an age of speed and control. We are an instant generation which wants immediate results. To gain quick results we continually improve our technology and expertise and our methods of control. We find it hard to wait for someone or some process that is outside our control.

But life and growth partake of mystery and both lie outside our control. In one of his parables Jesus describes how a farmer, having prepared the ground and planted the seed, now has to wait. 'Night and day, while he sleeps, when he is awake, the seed is sprouting and growing; how, he does not know' (Mk 4:27). Jesus touches on mystery with those words, 'how, he does not know'. Our modern farmer has made immense progress in understanding nature and improving farming techniques, but he is no closer to solving the mystery of life and growth. Prayer deals with this very mystery and demands patient waiting.

What happens while this farmer waits? Part of the mystery of growth is some kind of dying experience. 'Unless a wheat grain falls on the ground and dies, it remains only a single grain; but if it dies, it yields a rich harvest' (Jn 12:24). The growth of a personal love relationship is no exception to this rule. Some kind of dying has to take place here also. In our growing relationship of love with God, we will have to die to many of the false, childish ideas we may have had about God. We will have to allow God to be God and humbly surrender to his mystery. We can only have a proper love relationship with the true God Jesus revealed. We have to break the idol of the small God we have made in our image and likeness, the God who measures, who keeps a record of wrongdoing, who punishes, the God I can bribe with good behaviour, the God I can somehow control with ritual or prayer technique, the God I carry in my pocket like a charm. I will have to let this old God die so that I can meet the true God revealed by Jesus who invites me to rejoice with him in his Father. The God of Jesus will continually surprise me and win my heart.

One of the ways he will surprise me is by introducing me to my own true self. He will ask me to die to my false images of my own self. The more sincerely I can say to him, 'You are wonderful, so much more wonderful and beautiful than I ever imagined', the more he will open my eyes to see that I also am wonderful, since I am made by him in his image and likeness. He will ask me to surrender old, destructive self- images of inferiority, guilt and self-judgment, of self-hatred and of wishing to be someone else. He will invite me to see myself as he sees me, made in his image, sharing in the wonder and beauty of his mystery. Under his gentle, loving acceptance, a new self of unsuspected beauty can emerge in which I can humbly rejoice. And, finally, I can give a very special joy to the heart of God when I join the Psalmist in his prayer and, sincerely and happily, thank God 'for the wonder of myself' (Ps 139:14).

When these two kinds of death experience go together, dying to my false images of God and of myself, a wonderful new life of love can be born which will give deep, rich meaning to life. How many are disappointed because their lives are not more exciting, interesting or fulfilling? As the years slip by, many feel that their dreams have not been fulfilled. They feel in some way cheated that the circumstances of their lives have conspired to keep them small, insignificant and hidden. So many feel that they have done nothing worthwhile and perhaps wonder if it is because of their own inadequacy that their lives are apparently so mediocre. But such thoughts touch only the surface, the glamour, the appearances, those very areas which are highlighted by the mass media. We need to switch off this media propaganda for a while and get in touch with the deeper reality, with that which is truly life and truly valuable. We need to go past what we do to discover who we are. This discovery can be made in prayer with the help of God's Spirit.

All this takes time and involves waiting and, as we said, we do not find this easy, Patience and perseverance will always be needed in prayer. A love relationship takes time to grow. We cannot bypass time. Our instant culture presents a special challenge to those who want to grow in a prayer life. The desire for quick results has invaded even the world of relationships and love. We are impatient even in this world of mystery. We cannot wait for the slow, strong growth of love relationships. Much media propaganda suggests that we can build a quick, successful relationship as soon as we meet a compatible friend. Life says otherwise! A good relationship takes time and hard work. Time is needed to get to know each other and that ongoing discovery makes demands on patience, tolerance, forgiveness and mutual healing. No book, course or seminar on human relationships will give us the power to be unselfish and loving. Time, effort and grace are needed. But our age would like to have instant love, instant intimacy, which becomes synonymous with sexual discovery. And so only the body is touched. The surface, the externals, assume all importance. The real hidden beauty, mystery and wonder of the other person remains undiscovered.

I believe that this mentality can affect our prayer life. It can lead to false expectations, to disappointment and finally to our abandoning of prayer. In our relationship with God in prayer we can be impatient. We want quick results in spiritual experience, sweetness in prayer, evidence of God's special favour in daily life, a special providence protecting us from suffering, a quick victory over moral weakness. When these things do not happen and we continue to experience dryness and constant distraction in prayer time and see little effect of the prayer in our lives, we are tempted to give up. All the saints speak of darkness in prayer. We must be able to bear this patiently and perhaps be consoled a little by remembering that much significant growth takes place in the dark, unobserved by human eyes. The new baby undergoes its miraculous development in the darkness of the womb. The pearl grows in the enclosed darkness of the oyster shell. The seed breaks open in that dark hidden world within the womb of the earth and is nourished there. It is getting ready to emerge as new life, to release all the beauty that was hiding within it. Roots push down deep into the darkness of the earth to gain power and strength, to hold the tall tree upright and anchor it in time of storm. So prayer can nourish us in its darkness and anchor us in love to face life's storms.

We are not good at waiting, but life teaches us to wait for the things which are most worthwhile. We wait patiently for spring, for the first rains and the growth and life they bring. We wait for fruit to ripen, for flowers to unfold. We wait for the birth of a baby, for the healing of a wound, for the coming holidays, for love to grow. All these are gift – rain, growth, spring flowers, new life, healing, love. They are not under our control. We cannot hurry them. In prayer we wait with Christ on God. It's as simple as that.

20

GOD IS NOT OFFENDED

I was regretting the past and fearing the future. Suddenly my Lord was speaking, My name is 'I am.' He paused. I waited. He continued, When you live in the Past with its mistakes and its regrets, it is hard. I am not there. My name is not 'I was.' When you live in the Future, with its problems and fears, it is hard. I am not there. My name is not 'I will be'. When you live in this moment, it is not hard. I am here. My name is 'I am.'

These words remind us of what has been said about the richness and wonder of the present moment and of how prayer, by leading us into awareness of the present moment, puts us in touch with God and his peace and power. They also draw attention to a common human experience which is the source of much upset in prayer lives. I refer to our common tendency to allow the past and the future to invade the present and occupy much of our thoughts and emotional lives. In prayer we describe this problem with the word 'distractions'. I want to pray, to be in the Lord's presence, to give him my whole attention just now for this time of prayer, but after a few moments of recollection I can be totally distracted with thoughts about past happenings and about what is to come in the near or distant future. My body stays in a posture of prayer but my mind wanders through time and space. I have imaginary conversations with all kinds of people, conversations where I am always right and solve all problems! I dialogue with everyone except the good Lord himself whom I was supposed to encounter in this time of prayer.

Many good people are genuinely upset by this problem. They feel that their distracted prayer is unworthy of God. They feel ashamed and blame themselves. 'Here I have the privilege of entering God's holy presence. I believe in his great love for me and that he wants to bless me now in prayer. Yet after a few minutes I cease to pay attention to him. My mind wanders off to trivial matters, even to sinful thoughts and desires. And this continues to happen after years of prayer.' The first thing I say to these people is 'Congratulations! You are great to keep trying despite the painful awareness of your own poverty. You really want to love the Lord.' The inevitable temptation in this situation is to give up prayer. Here I offer a cautionary comment to those who think they should give up. Your upset at distractions may arise from a genuine respect for God. But it could also come from a subtle form of self-love and hurt pride. Why do distractions upset us? Are we upset because we think God is offended? Or could it be because distracted prayer is very unsatisfying and damaging to our pride? We don't like to be faced with our own poverty and nothingness. We want to be in control and to achieve something in the spiritual life. To give up prayer because of distractions could be a selfish decision, whereas to continue, despite this humbling experience, could be a sign of genuine love.

Is God offended by my distraction in prayer? I believe he is not the slightest bit offended. Rather he is pleased if I persevere despite the problem. We must be honest here. We will always experience these distractions. All spiritual writers on prayer agree that we cannot expect to pray without them. We spoke of growth in prayer. That does not mean that distractions will vanish in time. If we delude ourselves that they will disappear then we will conclude that our distractions are a sign of bad prayer and of our unworthiness and we will want to give up. Satan is the only one who will be pleased if we do so. Prayer is a way of loving. As we meet problems in loving, we will meet problems in prayer. We do not stop loving because of problems. Let us not stop praying.

Spiritual writers make a helpful distinction between 'intention' and 'attention' in prayer. They say 'intention' is in our power and under our control. But 'attention' is not. I can intend to spend the next hour with God in prayer, but I cannot guarantee that for the next hour all my attention will be on God only. I can say, 'For the next hour I will be with God in prayer.' I cannot say, 'For the next hour of prayer I will have no distractions.' I think the important question to ask is, 'Why do I come to God in prayer and why do I keep trying despite the torment of distractions?' The answer is that I believe in God's love. I hear his invitation and respond humbly in joyful hope. I seek the Lord and believe he is drawing me close to himself. I want this union. Some writers use the image of a river flowing to the sea. The deep hidden current of the river flows steadily to the sea which draws it. This is my desire for union with

God in prayer. At the same time the surface carries all kinds of flotsam and debris – our distractions.

One reason for our distractions is simply our human make-up. It is the whole person who comes to prayer – body, spirit, mind, senses, memory and emotions. These senses do not cease to function during prayer. They are in contact with many stimuli – sounds, smells, sights, bodily sensations. When stimulated they send signals to the mind and it wanders off. They trigger the memory, which starts up its own private video show. Such is the nature of the poor weak person who is invited to prayer. And the one who invites us is the eternal Mystery of God who is beyond all knowledge. We must not be naïve and think prayer will happen because we become still. Prayer does not happen, just as love does not happen. Silence does not conjure up God. But wonderful to say, and greatest of all miracles, this God seeks me and wants to uncover his face to me (Nb 6:26). So I can approach him in prayer with deep humility but with most joyful confidence. He will grant our heart's desire, the desire he implanted there. We recall the words of St Augustine: 'You have made us for yourself, O Lord, and our hearts are restless until they rest in you.'

Is there anything we can do about this problem of distractions? We can check and see if some are more culpable than others. What about the place of prayer? It may be a corner of my room. Do I use any symbol or object to help me focus – a crucifix, bible, picture, flower, candle? If not, do I at least remove from my vision the more distracting objects such as newspapers, etc? Is my chair comfortable but not so comfortable as to send me off to sleep? As I start my prayer, do I ask help from the Holy Spirit, the special helper God has given me for prayer (Rm 8:26)? When I begin, do I use any settling or awareness exercise to bridge the gap between my work and recreation and this new still place and time of prayer? I should not expect to be able suddenly to switch off my daily preoccupations and switch on God as I might change channels on my TV set.

It is helpful to spend the first five to ten minutes or more in some kind of awareness exercise. I gently become aware of my body, notice it, thank God for it and invite it to worship with me. We spoke elsewhere of an earlier spirituality which saw my body as an enemy of the spirit. But this body, which can be the source of many distractions in prayer, can also become a true partner in prayer. I can thank God for the different parts of the body and invite them to join me in thanks and worship. Let me pay special attention to my breathing. I let it become regular, breathing in the gift of life, breathing out my thanksgiving. I realise that this breath is gift. Gift suggests giver. I am being given the gift of breath, of life, by Another, by this God who loves me, seeks me, rejoices in me. I savour the absolute newness of this moment, this prayer, this activity of God in me. This activity is not a repetition of yesterday or any other day. It is something totally new. Such introductory reflections can lead me into prayer or may occupy much of the time of prayer.

Even when we do our best to dispose ourselves to prayer, the distractions will still come. We should be peaceful in handling them. Many find it helpful to make the distraction part of their prayer and to talk to God about the person, the activity or the problem which is distracting them. We can do this gently for some moments and then return to the main focus of our prayer, whether it be a gospel scene, a scripture word, an image, a mantra. Sometimes it happens that one particular distraction keeps recurring. It may centre on a person in my life or be related to some fear in my life regarding my health, an economic problem or a family problem. This is a special case and cannot be dealt with in time of prayer. It should be attended to in the ordinary way outside of prayer with the help of a friend or counsellor. This might even be the blessing the prayer brings. In a way it is God saying he is concerned. He wants me to have peace of soul and is saying he will be with the person I go to for help and advice. If I take these ordinary means, this distraction should lose some of its power to trouble me in prayer.

A rich source of distraction in prayer is noise. We cannot help hearing the variety of sounds from our surroundings, whether from within the house or the neighbourhood. Noise triggers off pictures and memories, and again the mind wanders. The advice here may seem strange but is very sound. We should not resist or try to ignore the sound but rather listen to it, allow it to become part of the prayer, and it will cease to distract us. A story from Anthony de Mello may help here. Brother Bruno is chanting the divine office when he is distracted by the croaking of a bullfrog outside the monastery window. He goes to the window and shouts out, 'Quiet. I'm praying.' The frog knows Bruno is a holy man and obeys. Bruno returns to prayer but has a new distraction. A voice is saying, 'Maybe God was as pleased by the croaking of the frog as he was by your singing of the Psalms.' Bruno asks how God could be pleased with such croaking, but the voice asks, 'Why do you think God invented the sound?' Poor Bruno gives in, goes to the window and shouts 'Sing'. The frog begins to croak and is now joined by a chorus of frogs. Bruno still hears the croaking but is not now disturbed by it. His heart is now more in harmony with creation.

Prayer is a faith exercise. It cannot be judged by the same criteria we apply to other human endeavours. Consolation and sweet feelings are not an indication of 'good' prayer. Consolation at prayer time can have several sources which are not necessarily spiritual. It can have its origin in good health, pleasant expectations or a good breakfast. Distractions and dryness are not signs of 'bad' prayer. To persevere despite such trials is a kind of purification of the spirit, but it is the very nature of purification that it is not recognised as such at the time. When I tell a spiritual director how poor my prayer is and he says it is all right, I just feel that he cannot have understood how poor my prayer really is! Prayer is hidden life. And it can be hidden in the deepest sense, even from myself.

Let us keep trying and leave the outcome to God. Since we deal with the infinite Mystery of God, prayer inevitably brings us face to face with our own poverty. This is both painful and healthy. It is painful because we like to be rich, even spiritually rich. It is healthy in the fullest sense of that word because it brings the fullness of life which Jesus promised for my whole person. Our poverty and emptiness open us to God's enriching, fulfilling love. Ultimately God wants me, not just my time. To surrender to him is the work of a lifetime. Slowly we become aware that prayer is chiefly God's work and activity and that, though we seek him, the eventual reality is not so much that we find him, but that he finds us.

21

MEET THE EXTENDED FAMILY

In August 1990, the hostage Brian Keenan was released after four years of captivity in Lebanon. In a TV interview after his release, he greatly impressed viewers with his calm bearing and forgiving spirit. In one memorable statement he rejected the idea of revenge and spoke of 'man's ability to form a fist to crush and destroy or to form a tool to write a book, play a piece of music, paint, make a friend. With the creative hand, people could contain, overcome and conquer the fist. This power in all of us is creative; it is passionate and it is unconquerable.' This was a wisdom born of suffering. The words he spoke and the accompanying gestures of one hand closed in a threatening fist and the other open and receptive were deeply impressive.

A popular song has the line, 'He's got the whole world in his hands.' These are the hands of God and, of course, they must be open. You cannot hold anything in a clenched fist except, perhaps, anger. We could adapt that song and sing: 'He's got the whole world in his heart'. Prayer is a journey with Christ into the heart of God. If prayer is genuine and truly leads into God's heart, then we must find the whole world there. 'God saw all he had made, and indeed it was very good' (Gn 1:31). True prayer is not a flight from the world, but an exploration of its deep, hidden meaning. Again, Paul's words come to mind and we can say to all creation, 'The life you have is hidden with Christ in God.' Prayer should lead us to appreciate this and so lead us into a new harmony with creation and a new respect and love for the world.

In the heart of God we must above all find people, all people. There is a false kind of prayer in which we seek to get away from people. In prayer, if we are with the true living God, Father of all, he will introduce us to the hidden lives of all our brothers and sisters. True prayer will lead us to a new way of seeing others which will bring us a new respect and love for them. People will become less of a burden, the more we take them into our love. Helder Camara asks, 'Do people weigh you down?' If they do, he says, 'Don't carry them on your shoulders. Take them into your heart.'

In his parable of the Last Judgment, when Jesus tells us he is present in the sick, hungry, naked, homeless, the prisoner, he is telling us that when we touch another person, we touch mystery, we touch God. Prayer brings us not only into the mystery of God but also into the mystery of people. A great modern apostle of compassionate love, Jean Vanier, speaks of his own deep need to be renewed in the prayer of solitude. But he also warns of a false solitude which could be a flight from people into selfish egoism. He writes, 'I discover more and more each day my need for these times of solitude in which I can rediscover others with more truth, and accept in the light of God my own weakness, ignorance, egoism and fear. This solitude does not separate me from others; it helps me love them more tenderly, realistically and attentively.'

A guru sits with his disciples and asks a question: 'How will you know the darkness of the night has ended and the brightness of day has come?' A disciple answers, 'I shall know the darkness of night is over and daylight is here when I look out my window and seeing a tree I can say, that is a mango tree, not a guava tree.' The guru shakes his head and invites another answer. A second disciple tries. 'I shall know the night has passed and day is here when I see an animal cross the road in the distance and I can say, "that is a dog, not a goat."' Wrong answer. Finally the guru gives his teaching. 'You will know the darkness of night is over and the brightness of day is here, when you look at the person beside you and recognise your sister or brother.' St John would have been happy with that answer. Speaking of the commandment of love, he says that when we walk in this commandment, 'the night is over and the real light is already shining. Anyone who claims to be in the light but hates his brother is still in the dark' (I Jn 2:8-9). True prayer leads me into the light where I can recognise the people around me as brother and sister. It leads me into the home of God's heart where he will introduce me to the rest of the family.

Then will come the discovery that the family of God is a great extended family and includes all creation. He's got the whole world in his hands and in his heart. I will be led into the mystery of my relationship not only with people but with all of God's creatures and can find myself recognising not only man and woman as brother and sister but also trees and flowers, sun and moon, birds and animals. This is the experience of many. St Augustine tells how in his search for God, he spoke to earth, sea, sun and other creatures, asking them if they could be God. They said no. He goes on, 'I said to all of these things which stood round the doors of my flesh: You have told me concerning my God that you are not he, give me at least some tidings of him. And they all cried out with a loud voice, "It is he that made us." My asking was my considering them, and their answering was the beauty I discovered in them.'

Francis of Assisi spoke with loving familiarity to Brother Sun and Sister Moon and to the creatures of the forest. There have been caricatures of this saint showing him as a sentimental nature-lover. But Francis was tough as steel, deeply in love with the living God and his Son Jesus. He entered into such compassionate experience of the sufferings of Christ that in ecstasy he was marked with the scars of the stigmata. And it was after this experience that he composed the 'Canticle of the Sun', his song of praise for Mother Earth, for sun, moon, wind, water and fire. St Ignatius of Loyola reminds us that each part of creation is a gift from God and that God is present in all these gifts, delighting us and loving us through them. This reflection invites us into new awareness of the great harmony of all creation of which we are part. Think again of Bruno the monk and how the croaking of the frog was a distraction for him in prayer as long as he saw the creature as distanced from God and in some way competing with him in worship. When he received the insight that the frog was God's creature delighting God with its own 'song', Bruno was in harmony with creation and could pray. We also noted how our bodies can join us and help us in prayer when we accept and love them and thus achieve personal harmony.

'God loved the world so much that he gave his only Son' (Jn 3:16). What world did he love that much? It was the world that he had made, the whole of creation, not just man and woman. And when Jesus walked in this world, he related to it with respect and love. All creatures, great and small, spoke to him of the Father and his love. He continually noticed the most insignificant creatures, thus reminding us that nothing is small or trivial in God's eyes. He speaks of the mustard seed, the smallest of all seeds, and uses it to teach us about God. He tells us that not one sparrow goes unnoticed by God and that every hair on our heads is numbered. He is aware of the scraps of food left over after the feeding of the crowd in the desert and orders that they be collected. We would have asked, 'Is there not plenty more where that came from?' He praises the tiny contributions of the widow to the temple collection and assures us elsewhere that even a cup of water given in love is noticed by God. Jesus finds mystery in the wild flowers, the bright plumage of birds, the flowing water, the lightning flash. He shows care and respect for the body. He declares opposition to sickness by repeated healings of body and spirit and is moved by people's hunger. All creatures, spirit or matter, great or small, are treated with reverence and love. Jesus is in harmony with his Father's creation.

By the incarnation God is again saying that his creation is good. His word of approval and love became flesh in Jesus. But there is a further depth to be explored in this relationship between God and the world, between Jesus and the world. St Paul suggests further wonder and mystery. To the Colossians he writes, 'Christ is the first-born of all creation, for in him were created all things in heaven and on earth; everything visible and everything invisible, all things were created through him and for him' (Col 1:15-16). Paul is saying that this world, this creation is to find its fulfilment and purpose in Jesus. He is to be the source of all harmony in the universe. He is the first-born of all this great extended family. The incarnation is not an improvisation in response to sin, a kind of contingency plan to undo the damage caused by sin. Christ has more meaning than that in God's eyes. This is something planned from eternity. 'He has let us know the mystery of his purpose, the hidden plan he so kindly made in Christ from the beginning, that he would bring everything together under Christ, as head, everything in the heavens and everything on earth' (Ep 1:9-10).

So we are all bound intimately together in Christ. He is the head of this great body of creation. In this body under him we are totally interdependent. The eye cannot say to the hand, 'I don't need you' (I Co 12:21). We all need each other, and this interdependence, this harmony, this one body refers not only to people needing other people, but to our needing our brothers and sisters, the sun, earth, sea, animal and vegetable creation. Lack of love for people can destroy a community. Lack of love and respect for the rest of the family of creation can destroy the wider extended family of creation. We are beginning to learn this lesson in our own day when modern progress has made the world small and put us so closely in touch with one another. We are beginning to realise now how much we can hurt or heal each other. If the eye cannot say to the hand, 'I don't need you', neither can we say to the sea or the forests, 'We don't need you.' And neither can one country or continent say to another, 'We don't need you.' A modern writer puts it this way: 'To say Japan has a pollution problem is like saying "your end of the boat is leaking".'

True prayer can lead us into this mystery of our being one family and can empower us to respond to the challenge of modern progress and technology. Prayer is not a flight from the world but an exploration of its depths. It leads us not to despise the world but to love it, the world which Jesus knew and loved, the world he gave his life for. Our prayer must lead us into his heart, so that we share his love for the world and so that we too in some way may be prepared to give our lives for this world. There is an urgent need today to rediscover love and respect for creation. It takes little thought to realise that we have not loved the world, that we have not respected this great gift to us. We dominate and exploit it. We contaminate the earth and pollute the atmosphere in a totally selfish way. We have lost the spirit of reverence and gratitude for the gift of creation. We separate the gift from the Giver, the creation from the Creator, in our selfish desire for quick gain and total domination. We have, in our day, reached a point where we can annihilate ourselves and all creation.

We must recover a sense of wonder and mystery and a sense of the dignity of our vocation to work with the Creator to develop creation and make it an instrument of love. Creation was not finished in seven days. It is ever ongoing. Jesus says, 'My Father is always working and so am I' (Jn 5:17). And the Psalmist reminds us that when we get tired and retire to rest our working God is still active. 'He provides for his beloved as they sleep' (Ps 127:2). We recalled God's presence in the mystery of the growth of the seed. While the farmer waits, the seed grows, 'he knows not how'. We must recover this sense of wonder at God present and at work in creation. There is more to the world than meets the eye, more than X-ray or microscope can reveal. When science dissects and analyses the different parts of the creation, it has not understood the world nor exhausted its meaning. We can take a watch apart, lay out its every part on the table and then put it together again and we have a watch. Not so with creation, which is more than the sum of its parts. It too has its own hidden life, hidden with Christ in God.

22

STONES WILL CRY OUT

'The fool says in his heart, "There is no God"' (Ps 53:1). This word of the Psalmist is echoed in another word from an eastern holy man who says, 'When the wise man points to the moon, the fool sees only his finger.' In these sayings the word 'fool' is not meant to be offensive or insulting. It denotes the person who lacks 'wisdom', especially the wisdom to see past signs and externals to the hidden life and beauty in our world and, especially, to recognise the source and origin of it all, namely God. God communicates much of his beauty and glory to us through the sign language of creation. We are meant to look past the signs to the reality towards which they point.

On a journey we expect to meet signposts on the road before we reach our destination. Before we reach the town, hospital or airport, we expect to see signs pointing the way. It would be very awkward if someone put up a sign and there was no corresponding reality further down the road! And on our part how foolish we would be if we stopped at the signpost, imagining we had arrived! In a way that is what people have always been tempted to do with the signs God places to lead us to him. They admire the pointing finger. We call this idolatry. We identify the signs, the creation, with God, and we stop and worship. In earlier days people did this with trees, mountains, the sun. Today we are more sophisticated but we still have our idols. Money, power and pleasure are some of our idols today. Even religion, which forbids idolatry, can fall into the trap and give to some sacred sign, dogma, ritual or holy book, the status and worship due to God alone. We must travel past all signs, even religious signs, to the Mystery they signal. Idolatry forsakes truth. Isaiah picks up a carved idol and says, 'What I have in my hand is nothing but a lie' (Is 44:40).

The day after the miracle of the feeding of the crowd in the desert the people flock around Jesus. He knows that they now follow him for bread. He says something to them which used to puzzle me. 'I tell you most solemnly, you are not looking for me because you have seen the signs but because you had all the bread

105

you wanted to eat' (Jn 6:26). Jesus seems to say, 'You did not see the signs yesterday', but they were present and had eaten and had seen the signs. I believe now that Jesus is saying, 'You saw the sign yesterday but did not identify it as a sign pointing to a greater reality. When I fed you with bread it was meant to be a sign but you mistook it for the reality.' We do not live on bread alone. We have other deeper hungers which Jesus has come to satisfy. 'Do not work for food that cannot last, but work for food that endures to eternal life, the kind of food the Son of Man is offering you' (Jn 6:27).

When we do see signs as signs and let them lead us past themselves to the reality towards which they point, then we enter a world of mystery and wonder. When we let the creation shout out to us as it did to St Augustine, 'He made us. We have our beauty from him', then we enter a world of beauty and joy which moves us to that most true expression of our relationship with God, the prayer of praise. The prayer of praise responds to God as God. Praise is worship given only to the true and living God. Praise was never offered to idols. People offered only flattery to idols, an insincere 'praise' offered to win favour and keep the gods on their side. But when we find the true God we know that he is always on our side and that he is all beauty, love and power. Then our whole being is moved to praise. It is not just respect. It is simply the overflow of joy at realising how wonderful he is. It is spontaneous. No one will have to tell us to praise. No one has to hold up a sign marked 'Alleluia', as signs marked 'Applause' were once held up to TV audiences in case they might not clap at the right time!

The prayer of praise tells not only about the wonder of God but also something wonderful about ourselves. Let us ask, 'What do we usually praise in life?' We praise things which are good and beautiful. We praise courage and kindness in people, the beauties of nature, a good book, inspiring music. Now ask a deeper question. Why do we praise these things? We praise them because something in us recognises beauty, truth and goodness. We are not strangers to each other. We have met before. I wonder where! The good, true and beautiful touch something deep within us. There is an echo and we experience a sense of harmony and we know joy. And God who is the source of all goodness, beauty and truth smiles and says to us, 'I told you that you were made in my image and likeness.' A disciple comes to his master and asks,

'Master, where do mountains, trees, stars and the sea come from?' The master pauses, looks at the disciple and replies, 'Where does your question come from?' The answer to both these questions is the same. The beauty and wonder of the world come from God and our power to recognise it comes from the same God within us.

The prayer of praise has another important teaching for us. Notice that sincere praise always leads to a desire to share. When you discover something good and beautiful, your first instinct is to want to share it. You open the hall door in the morning and there is a great rainbow spanning the sky. Instinctively you shout back into the house, 'Come and see the rainbow!' When you hear a new song or discover a good book, you want to tell your friends. If on your way to work you witness an act of bravery, for example someone risking her life to save a child about to be run over, you will want to share the experience with all at work. And always the joy increases when we share. This brings us deeper into the mystery of God and ourselves. If, when we are at our best, we like to share good things, the reason is that the true nature of the God in whose image we are made is a sharing God. God's very being is to share and this may help us understand better the central mysteries of our faith, the Trinity, the Creation and the Incarnation. All these have to do with sharing, with communicating goodness, beauty and love.

The greatest secret God shared with us about his own inner self was that he was one God but three persons, Father, Son and Spirit. In revealing his wonder of the Trinity, God was not offering us a mathematical puzzle. He was not saying, 'Now I will tell you something very puzzling about myself. You will not understand it, but you have to accept and believe it.' No. Rather, God was acting like a friend who wants to share his deepest secret with us and the secret is that he is not a distant, cold and lonely God, but a community of love. He is telling us that the very heart and centre of reality is love and sharing, is relationship. And, further, this inner mutual love of the Trinity does not remain in an enclosed circle but joyfully breaks out and overflows into creation. This creation is the joyful outpouring of the life, love and beauty of God in an amazing variety of being. The creation is the song and dance of the Trinity. We are the pinnacle of the creation. We alone are made in the image of this God. It is no wonder that in our best moments we can recognise beauty and love and act in a loving and sharing way.

The creation did not exhaust God's love or his gifts. In the Incarnation he gives the ultimate, incredible gift of himself in Jesus his Son. Gifts are the lover's sign language and they say, 'I really want to give you myself.' And so our God in Jesus gives himself, even to Calvary. He shares our humanity to the full so we may share his divinity. And to help us enter into these miracles of love and appreciate them, the Father and Son give us their own Holy Spirit, who is the Spirit of joy, love and celebration. It is this Spirit who moves us to the prayer of praise. We need not be surprised that when the Spirit came at Pentecost there was a great outburst of praise.

The old catechism answer said that we were created to praise, reverence and serve God. Notice, praise is first. For many years this prayer of praise did not have its rightful place in my life, chiefly because I did not appreciate the love, goodness and beauty of God. I saw prayer as a duty to be done to please God and win his favour. There was a suggestion that God was in some way benefitting from my praise and would be poorer if I failed to praise him. Then came the realisation that I was the one who was blessed when I praised God. The prayer of praise was just one more gift from this sharing God. The gift of praise draws me into God's own inner life. The Spirit leads me to share in the celebration of life, joy and beauty which is God himself. The Trinity is no longer a teaching standing outside of me to be studied and understood. It is the communication of the fullness of God's life. It is the spring of living water and I am invited to drink and be renewed.

Jesus himself experienced a deep joy given by the Spirit when he was sharing his Father's love with us. 'It was then that, filled with joy by the Holy Spirit, he said, "I bless you, Father, Lord of heaven and of earth, for revealing these things to mere children"' (Lk 10:21). At the Last Supper he again refers to this joy: 'I have told you this so that my own joy may be in you and your joy may be complete' (Jn 15:11). Shortly before this, on Palm Sunday, the excited crowd was swept away by great enthusiasm and 'joyfully began to praise God at the top of their voices' (Lk 19:37). They broke branches from trees and threw garments on the road. The Pharisees were angry. 'Some Pharisees in the crowd said to him, "Master, check your disciples," but he answered, "I tell you, if these keep silence the stones will cry out"' (Lk 19:39-40). Jesus knew the human heart well and was aware that there was much surface emotion here, and that these people singing praise now could easily turn against him. But still, in defending the crowd that day, he testified to the deep reality that the goodness and wonder of his Father's love did merit joyful, enthusiastic praise. Today, all over the world, we repeat, daily in the Eucharist that Palm Sunday song of praise, 'Hosanna in the highest. Blessed is he who comes in the name of the Lord. Hosanna in the highest.'

The prayer of the Mass says it is right and fitting that we should 'always and everywhere' give praise and thanks to God. We have been saying that praise is a response to the beauty and goodness of God. Now let us face reality and admit that the goodness and beauty of God are not obvious 'always and everywhere'. We spoke earlier about suffering, sickness, injustice, sin. Goodness and beauty are terribly obscured here. Can I still praise God even in such situations? The answer has to be yes, because God is still God. He is still present and at work, forgiving, healing, re-creating. To praise him now when all external circumstances hide his beauty and his loving presence is an exercise of deep faith.

This spirituality of continuing to give praise to God in time of suffering has transformed people and situations. We must be careful how we understand such prayer and what is going on in our hearts when we praise God in the presence of suffering and evil. We are not making light of the suffering and we are not compromising with the evil. Nor are we absolving ourselves from our responsibility to do all we can to remove the suffering and overcome evil. What then are we saying? We are confessing that God is still God. In this suffering he is not defeated. His power is not diminished by the misfortunes of this person or that group. He is not far away but is present. He is loving and stronger than the suffering or the evil. I continue to praise him because I am certain that his love will prevail and that he will deliver me and bring good out of this situation. I am thanking him in advance. If I trust and do my best with his help to overcome the suffering, while patiently uniting my pain with that of Christ, then the power of God will be seen and the risen life will be experienced. In continuing to praise God in time of suffering, I am saying to God:

> You are God always and everywhere even, in the darkest moments. I do not understand why this is happening But I know that I am in your hands and

109

you are in control. I know you love me and your love is strong and everlasting.

So I will continue to praise you always and everywhere.

23

HIDDEN BEAUTY REVEALED

'God does not see as man sees; man looks at appearances but Yahweh looks at the heart' (I S 16:7). This book has been inviting us to see as God sees. It asks us not to be captivated by appearances. So, we have been exploring the heart of the matter, our hidden life. We do this with reverence and wonder. The word 'hidden' does not suggest something poor, inferior or less noteworthy, but, rather, the opposite. It points us to what is most true, rich, beautiful and lasting. This hidden life, which is our love relationship with God, is what gives all value, meaning and wonder to our lives. This life we have reflected on is built, founded and rooted in Jesus Christ who shares it with us. We are not merely exploring our inner consciousness. We are not seeking some kind of greater self-awareness or self-fulfilment apart from this Jesus. This hidden life, with all its wonder and beauty, gets its meaning from this historical person, this Jesus who walked on earth. He was a full human person like us and he was also the Son of God. He is Jesus, the same yesterday, today, forever. We walk with him on holy ground. It is faith ground, but solid ground.

Staying close to him, we are then invited by God to look beyond our hidden selves to the wider human family and then further beyond to the great extended family of creation. Again we are asked to go past externals and appearances, to see the heart of creation and discover the mystery of God always present and at work renewing, nourishing and re-creating. And in some mysterious way all this dynamic is again bound up with Christ. We recall St Paul's words, 'Christ is the image of the unseen God, and the first-born of all creation, for in him were created all things in heaven and on earth, everything visible and everything invisible – all things were created through him and for him' (Col 1:15-16). The poet Patrick Kavanagh sees children picking up daisies and primroses, partial revelations of God's truth and beauty. He longs to see all God's beauty together in one great bouquet. But he knows this cannot be, because, as he says, 'God is not all in one place complete.' St Paul would say, 'God is all in one person complete', the person of Jesus.

All this reflection invites us to a new appreciation of prayer, of our need for stillness and solitude so we can get past the lure of the externals, past the appearances, and discover the heart of people and creation which God always sees. This prayer is clearly not an escape from reality but an exploration of its depths. It is not a drug or a painkiller to help us forget for a while, rather it brings deep healing and promotes growth. It puts us in touch with the wellspring of life which is clean, refreshing, lifegiving water. This prayer is not a running away from work and responsibility but an invitation to join God in his daily creative activity. We do not try in prayer to get God to do our will, but we joyfully open ourselves to his will, which is not to be imagined as some immutable blueprint fixed from all eternity which we are supposed to find and conform to. God's will is God's love working out daily in this great creation and ready for all the contingencies that can arise from our weakness and failure. In one of his retreats Carlo Martini writes, 'God has no cosmic programme worked out in advance. Jesus did not present a Christianity so planned that it cannot stop to seek out a lamb or a silver coin or a child who has left the family home.'

There is no fixed cosmic programme, no immutable blueprint. Only one thing is fixed and immutable for eternity and that is that God is love and desires all people and creation to be saved and brought to fullness of life through Christ. How that works out in practice can involve trial and error and lots of mistakes from us his co-creators. God was well aware of our human limitations and weakness when he chose us and chose the Incarnation. He can cope with that. God can cope with our poor planning. What he cannot cope with is our refusal to love. In prayer we seek to discover what God wants us to do now for our brothers and sisters and all creation. When we seek, we will be given the guidance and creative power of the Holy Spirit to bring harmony, unity and love to creation.

One day Jesus, after telling his disciples that they would be badly treated just as he was being treated, spoke a word of consolation to them. He told them that these and other things which puzzled them and were so obscure would one day become clear. He said, 'Do not be afraid. For everything that is now covered will be uncovered, and everything now hidden will be made clear' (Mt 10:26-27). We can apply these words to our theme. The hidden life we are speaking about will one day be revealed in all its wonder and beauty. How will this happen and when? We go back to the image of the seed. A dying experience must precede the revealing of the new life and

112

beauty hidden in the seed. It is the same rule for us. We all move towards the doorway of death leading to this promised revealing. This movement to death has nothing to do with a certain time. Again we judge by appearances and see the death of the young as a kind of frustration. Not so with God. In a sense we grow younger, not older. Jesus says heaven is for children. When we are young enough, he will call us.

For the majority, the growth is slow and spaced over time. We speak of growing older. Hopefully we will accept the wisdom expressed in the 'Desiderata': 'Take kindly the counsel of the years, gracefully surrendering the things of youth.' Hopefully, as we get more in touch with the deeper hidden life, we will resist the temptation to feel that life has less meaning because we can do less. That is the deception I have been trying to expose in this book, the deception which equates meaning with doing and achieving. As the years run on and time runs out and there are fewer horizons, our movement into old age should not be a movement into regret and disappointment but into greater awareness of new meaning, into expectation and joyful hope. The slowing down and weakening simply means that the next chapter of life is approaching. The external body of the seed has to break up precisely so that all the potential life and beauty of the flower may emerge.

And in the process of growing old, let us again love our bodies, these faithful friends who have journeyed life with us. They will weaken and deteriorate with the years. But their own time of glory approaches when their youth will be renewed like the eagle's (Ps 103:5). Some poor bodies go through very painful and traumatic final days. We see once lovely bodies ravaged by cancer and AIDS. We see others brutalised, tortured or abused and maybe left to rot and decompose unmourned. We hate to see such bodies in photographs and documentary films, bloated, maimed, burnt and bereft of all respect. We are sad to see the pitiful remains uncovered in mass graves in many parts of the world, those terrifying legacies of evil too common in history. We are filled with sadness as we imagine how these people must have died. But it will be all right. God does not judge by appearances. He loves each body he created and will bring them all from such death, decay and abuse into glory and immortality and incredible new beauty. St Paul says that if our poor little seed can become a beautiful flower, what about our poor mortal bodies? (1 Co 15:35).

All things are possible to God. Indeed, the body of his own

113

Beloved Son was in a very bad state that Friday on Calvary. 'Without beauty, without majesty we saw him, no look to attract our eyes; a thing despised and rejected by men, a man to make people screen their faces' (Is 53:3). But his Father caught him and took him into his arms and in that love embrace his body is glorified and its beauty renewed. Will this Father not do for all his children what he did for this first-born Son?

Finally, my own deepest hidden self has also to be revealed in all its beauty. It too in its day of revealing will have to shed all externals, all appearances. I do not refer to shedding the body because it too is destined for glory and immortality. I refer to all the other trappings which the self sought in the hope of finding more meaning and making itself more beautiful. Not recognising its own beauty already given, it used all kinds of make-up to appear more attractive. I speak of all the lies and pretence, all the success and achievement, the wealth and possessions, the social status and prestige. All this must be shed and left so that the true beauty of the self may be seen. We have seen art experts working on a rare and precious painting, gently and lovingly stripping off layers of dust and paint that have accumulated over the years so that the original beauty may be revealed. 'We are God's work of art, created in Christ Jesus' (Ep 2:10). Then all those false identities imposed on me by others have to be dropped, all the masks I wore, all the roles I assumed to please parents, teachers, the neighbours, the Church, my peers, must be thrown off and left behind so that I can find myself. I imagine that most of us will throw off these masks with a great sigh of relief in death.

And what is left after all this shedding? In an old comedy film, the comic hero, dressed as a highwayman, holds up a coach. He wears a large black mask. But, as we might expect, he bungles the robbery. The coach driver gets the better of him, points his pistol at him and snarls, 'Take off that mask!' To which the hero replies, 'I can't. I have nothing on underneath!' Is that not our fear in life? We wear masks because we feel we have no value or beauty within us. What is left in death when we remove all the masks? We can answer that what is left is that which alone is beautiful, that which alone lasts and never fades, the mystery of love. Paul says, 'Love does not come to an end' (I Co 13:8).

In this well-known passage on love, Paul has an intriguing word: 'Now we are seeing a dim reflection in a mirror; but then we shall be seeing face to face. The knowledge that I have now is imperfect;

but then I shall know as fully as I am known' (I Co 13:12). When Paul says 'I shall know as I am known', I presume he means 'as I am known by God.' He is saying, 'I will see myself as God sees me.' And, as we have been told, 'Yahweh sees the heart.' In that moment of truth I shall look into the only mirror that can show my true likeness, my real self, my hidden self, the mirror of God's eyes. And Christ will be there beside me, to rejoice with me, and the Holy Spirit will be the light enabling me to see.

> Now the life you have is hidden with Christ in God.
> But when Christ is revealed – and he is your life –
> you too will be revealed in all your glory with him.
>
> Col 3:3-4